New Business Opportunities

JEFFRY A. TIMMONS
Babson College &
Harvard Business School

New Business Opportunities

Getting to the Right Place at the Right Time

BRICK HOUSE PUBLISHING COMPANY
Acton , Massachusetts

Dedication

To the"overprivileged kids" and adults of Third Machias and Okemo

Toby, Samantha, Jesseca, Hannes and Anya
Willie, Charlie and Andy
Sayer, Kezia and Kaley
Sara, Sarah and Howard
Jake, Jack and Diana
Truman and Beep
Karla and Bok

You have given me the greatest opportunity of all:
The endless memories and joys on many occasions
of being at the right place at the right time,
with you, at my favorite places.

Library of Congress Cataloging-in-Publication Data

Timmons, Jeffry A.

New business opportunities : getting to the right place at the right time / Jeffry A. Timmons

p. cm.

ISBN 0-931790-90-5 : ISBN 0-931790-91-3 (pbk.)

1. New business enterprises. 2. Entrepreneurship. I. Title.

HD62 . 5 . T548 1990 89-9721

658. 1 ' 1—dc20 CIP

Contents

Preface

We are in the midst of what I call the "The Silent Revolution," an unusual revolution of the human spirit and the marketplace: a discovery of the *extraordinary power of the entrepreneurial process*. By creating or recognizing and seizing opportunities, by providing imagination, tenacity and leadership, and by insisting on the higher ground of ethical and square dealing, successful entrepreneurs play for the long haul. In this complicated process they create and allocate value and benefits for individuals, groups, organizations and society.

Opportunity creation and recognition is at the heart of the entrepreneurial process. The very molecules of economic development begin here, with the idea or concept for a new business venture: a way to do things better, filling a gap or need, seeing what others do not. But there is an *enormous difference between an idea and a good business opportunity.* Knowing what those differences are, how to evaluate them, and ways to pursue them are crucial to entrepreneurial success. This is the focus of this book.

The entrepreneurial roots and backbones of economic progress are now being discovered worldwide, and show unprecedented promise of a sustained, global entreprenuerial wave, including China and other eastern bloc nations. Lighting the flame of the entrepreneurial spirit empowers nations and peoples with "the knowledge and ability to fish, rather than just giving them a fish."

Among the adult working population in the U.S. about one in eight is self-employed, and it can be said that a cultural imperative exists in the minds of millions of other Americans: the entrepreneurial dream of working for oneself, of "growing up big." And it is no wonder, once you discover how self-employed feel about themselves and their work lives, and what the the economic rewards are. Uniformly, these self-employed persons report the highest levels of personal satisfaction, challenge, pride and remuneration. As a lot they love their work because it is invigorating, energizing and meaningful. Compared to managers and those working for others, as many as three times more never plan to retire. They seem to love the "entrepreneurial game" for the game's sake. The vast majority of the two million "millionaires" in the U.S. in 1987 have accumulated their wealth through entrepreneurial acts of self-employment.

What may be more surprising is that even graduates of the Harvard Business School—long thought of as the "West Point for the Fortune 500"—thrive on this entrepreneurial dream: about one-third end up working for themselves, and the vast majority of all graduates ten years after graduation work for companies employing fewer than one thousand people. Further evidence of just how wide and deep is the quest for entrepreneurship is reflected by the readership of the *Harvard Business Review:* about 70% are owners, executives or managers of firms with fewer than one thousand employees. And among the students at HBS, nearly 90% say they have the entrepreneurial dream of self-employment. A recent survey of Fortune 500 CEOs showed two dominant activities they considered the most prestigious: first, owning or investing in a small company, and second, international travel. One has to ask: what is going on here?

The rebirth of the "entrepreneurial wave" in America in the past decade has brought unprecedented benefits not just to individuals but to society as a whole. Entrepreneurs, it turns out, are the fuel, engine and throttle for the economic backbone of the country. Consider the following:

• About 1.3 million new enterprises from one-person operations and up will be launched in the U.S. in 1989. Contrast this with perhaps 200,000 a year 25 years ago, and 600,000 a year as recently as 1983.

• Today there are about 19 million enterprises of all kinds in the U.S., and it is estimated that there will be 30 million by the year 2000. By 1985 there were nearly four million enterprises owned by women in the U.S., and between 1980 and 1985 the rate at which women were creating businesses was two to five times greater than all others. By the year 2000 40% or more of all businesses will be owned by one or more women, dramatic evidence of "the silent revolution."

• The U.S. has the *same number* of people working in manufacturing jobs today as we did in 1966. Yet, since 1966 the nation's economy has added 30 million new jobs! What is more, virtually all of the net new jobs created in this country come from new and expanding firms—not from the large, established companies. One recent study reported than just 7% of these new and expanding ventures accounted for a remarkable 118% of all the net new jobs in the early 1980s. In 1987 employment in seven million small firms grew three times faster than employment in the 500 largest companies in the nation, according to American Express.

• Since World War II, half of all innovations and 95% of all radical innovations have come from new and smaller firms. Innumerable innovations and industries began this way: the heart pacemaker, the microcomputer, overnight express packages, the quick oil change, fast food, the oral contraceptive, the x-ray machine, and hundreds of others.

• Just 37 individual entrepreneurs inducted into the Babson College Academy of Distinguished Entrepreneurs in 1977–88 have created and/or built companies—many from nothing—to combined sales which would place their thirty-seven companies as the *20th largest GNP* in the world. Their names are entrepreneurial legends: Royal Little, An Wang, Frank Perdue, Ken Olsen, Sochio Honda, Ray Kroc, Fred Smith, Nolan Bushnell, Trammel Crow, Willard Marriott, Ed Lowe, Wally Amos, H. R. Bloch, Don Burr, John Cullinane, Rupert Murdoch, Peter Sprague, John Templeton, and others with equal deeds but lesser familiarity.

• The entrepreneurial fever has also spread to colleges and high schools in recent years, and now shows promise of gaining the attention of administrators and teachers in elementary schools. Over 400 colleges and universities offer courses in new ventures and entrepreneurship, compared to as few as 50 in 1975.

• Between $50 and $60 billion of informal risk capital exists in our economy, almost entirely coming from self-made entrepreneurs called "angels."

• Another $30 billion of venture capital funds are available from professional sources seeking to back small company entrepreneurs with big ambitions—Apple Computer, Federal Express, Lotus Software, Digital Equipment Corporation, Data General, and the like started with just such sources. Such funds are now a worldwide phenomenon, including the United Kingdom, Scandanavia, Western Europe, Spain, Kenya, Brazil, Australia, Philippines, Japan, Korea and others.

• For the first time ever, in June and July, 1987, 46 senior policy makers, researchers, entrepreneurs and executives from 26 countries met at the Salzburg Seminar in Austria for an eight-day session entitled "Entrepreneurship," led by Professor Howard H. Stevenson of Harvard. Only three Americans attended. The rest looked like a United Nations contingent: China, Russia, Romania, Turkey, Norway, West Germany, Poland, Scotland, Ireland, England, Egypt, Greece, Yugoslavia, Spain, Portugal, Sweden, Netherlands, Belguim, Austria, Malaysia, Singapore and others.

• Entrepreneurship is not just the domain of new and small firms. It can also happen in old and large companies (though we see it far less frequently), in slower growing and even troubled companies, in profit-seeking and non-profit organizations, and in the eastern, western and developing economies. But what may be most singnificant of all: it also can *fail to occur*.

This book has two principal roots, going back over twenty years. Since 1971, and earlier doing doctoral research at the Harvard Business School, I have been immersed in the world of entrepreneurs and the start-up, development, financing and harvesting of new and growing (and sometimes shrinking) companies: as a student, researcher, teacher and scholar, and as an investor, advisor, director and founding shareholder.

In 1971 I became a founding shareholder of Venture Founders Corporation, a Boston venture capital firm with subsidiaries in the U.K. and Belguim, with over $65 million under management. I worked closely with VFC from 1971-82 in developing ways to identify, evaluate and finance seed-stage and stage-up ventures. This was an important testing ground for applying and refining my approaches to launching and growing higher potential ventures.

Through my own firm, Curtis-Palmer & Company, Inc., which I founded in 1981, my clientele have included presidents and partners of venture capital firms and emerging companies in the U.S., U.K. and

Sweden, including Investkontakt & Svetab, Venture Founders Corporation, Zero Stage Capital, Venture Economics (publisher of *Venture Capital Journal*), Vlasic Foods (part of Campbell Soup) and The Sunmark Companies, a $160M+ private firm in St. Louis recently acquired by Nestle.

In 1981–82 I accepted a full-time assignment in Stockholm with one of the first venture capital firms there.

In 1984, as the first outside member of of the partnership committee of Cellular One in Boston, I became actively involved in starting and building the first independent car phone company in New England. In 1987 I became a founding shareholder and director of Boston Communications Group (BCG) which owns and operates cellular phone systems in southern Maine and New Hampshire, cellular phone installation and service centers, a cellular-credit card phone company and other telecommunications ventures.

Since 1985 I have assisted Ernst & Young's national Privately Owned Emerging Business Group to develop and implement professional development programs for partners in this leading Big Eight accounting firm, including Emerging Businesses & Entrepreneurship, and Financing Alternatives. This effort is now expanding to E&Y International in a similar effort for Canada and the United Kingdom.

In 1988 I joined the Advisory Board of Bridge Capital Investors, a $150 million bridge fund in Teaneck, N.J., which specializes in providing growth capital for emerging companies with sales in the $5-100 million range.

Of particular note is that these investing activities have spanned a range of high, low, and no technology businesses, and product and service businesses in the U.S., Canada, U.K. and Europe.

As a product of these experiences, *New Business Opportunities* is the second of three related books. *The Entrepreneurial Mind* was the first, and *Planning and Financing the New Venture* will appear later in 1989. This book and its two companions are rooted in both real-world applications and nearly two decades of refinement in the classroom. The content and material have won accolades from experienced MBAs, college seniors and hundreds of founders and owners of new and emerging companies pursuing their entrepreneurial dreams. Much of what is here is has been tempered and enhanced by my working directly with these entrepreneurs and entrepreneural firms—and usually while risking both my reputation and my wallet.

This book is a direct descendant of my earlier book, *New Venture Creation,* which has been become a leading textbook for courses in entrepreneurship and starting new ventures worldwide, and according to the *Wall Street Journal* (October 1987), a "textbook classic."

The Entrepreneurial Mind addresses what makes entrepreneurs tick and what they do—and avoid—to get the odds of success in their favor. How do they convert their dreams to tangible visions and to commercial realities? What do successful entrepreneurs do differently that enables them not only to survive but to "grow up big"? How do these entrepreneurs think and act? What are their winning strategies and approaches? How do they do their homework? What do they pay a lot of attention to—and know they can ignore?

The answers too these questions unlock part of the mystery of entrepreneurship. Once you know how winning entrepreneurs think, act and perform, then you can establish goals to practice emulating those actions, attitudes, habits and strategies. Certainly, the book does not pretend to know how to "make silk purses out of sows ears," but it has received quite favorable comments from numerous world-class entrepreneurs, including:

Peter J. Sprague, Chairman, National Semiconductor Corporation: "Your book is a revelation. You could have saved me a great deal of trouble and money if you had written it twenty years ago!"

J.W. Marriott, Jr, Chairman & President, Marriott Corporation: "Truly outstanding! Congratulations to you on your fine contribution to the society of entrepreneurs."

Royal Little, Late Founder and Chairman, Textron Corporation and Narragansett Capital: "I was tremendously impressed with the thoroughness with which you covered this complicated subject."

New Business Opportunities is aimed at "getting you to the right place at the right time." With 20-20 hindsight, and oversimplification, most people think it is just a matter of coincidence. Savvy, successful entrepreneurs (even if they have not read *The Entrepreneurial Mind*!) know it isn't nearly so easy. There is literally an unlimited number of ideas for products, services, processes and software.

Unsuccessful entrepreneurs typically equate an idea with an opportunity. Successful entrepreneurs know a good opportunity is more than just another good idea. Judging by small-firm failure statistics—as many as 9 out of 10 new firms fail in ten years—most of these "good ideas" do not work out. What may surprise you, even big companies do not fare any better: only about 1 in 10 of the new products brought to the shelves of America's supermarkets survive more than one year. And this is usually after months and millions of dollars spent on market research and testing.

What is a good opportunity? Why do a select few inherently have much greater upside potential than all the rest? Why and how do successful entrepreneurs often find the best opportunities amid the noise, chaos, confusion, competitive vacuums and contradictions of a turbulent and imperfect marketplace? How can you find such opportunities? Or create one? Would you recognize one when you see it? How can you determine whether the opportunity will last? Is it the right one for you? Does it have what I call "forgiving and rewarding economics"? Can you determine to what extent it will add or create value, and thereby actually fill a customer need? Do you know what to say 'no' to? What are the things to look for and look out for, in order to get the odds of success and the reward-risk balance in your favor?

The answers to these questions will help you to think big and avoid wild-goose chases. Judging by some early feedback from some of America's top entrepreneurs, *New Business Opportunities* is on the right track. Consider these comments:

"As practical as it is logical. New Business Opportunities is a bible for the entrepreneur." Roger A. Enrico, President and Chief Executive Officer, Pepsi-Cola Company.

"Timmons takes the mystery and magic out of that foreign word, 'entrepreneur,' and directs us to reality, to the living, working world. As he does this he magnifies that word with meaning and gives useful direction." Trammell Crow, Trammell Crow Company.

"Your book reminds us that running a business in today's world is to be deeply aware of market trends, the barriers to new entry, capital requirements, the need for expanding new products, and managing the unpredictable business environment." M. Gilbert Trigano, Chairman and CEO, Club Med.

"I greatly enjoyed reading your book. *New Business Opportunities* is a reference book for all entrepreneurs and should be on every entrepreneurial team's desk." Bert W. M. Twaalfhoven, International Entrepreneur, Industrialist and Venture Capitalist.

Jeffry A. Timmons
Harvard, Massachusetts
August 1989

About the Author

Jeffry A. Timmons is nationally and internationally known for his work in new ventures, venture capital, venture financing and entrepreneurship. He is currently the first holder of both the Frederic C. Hamilton Professorship at Babson College and the Class of 1954 Professorship at the Harvard Business School. He joined Babson in 1982 , as Paul T. Babson Professor, and has served as Director of the Center for Entrepreneurial Studies and the Price-Babson College Fellows Program. He has developed and teaches courses on starting new ventures and financing entrepreneurial ventures, and the Entrepreneurial Management Program for the presidents and executives of emerging businesses.

In addition to the practical experience noted above, he has conducted research in entrepreneurship on new and emerging firms and venture financing, which has resulted in nearly one hundred papers and articles in such publications as *Harvard Business Review* and *Journal of Business Venturing*, and in the proceedings of national and international conferences, including *Frontiers of Entrepreneurship Research* (1981–89). He is also quoted in publications such as *Wall Street Journal, INC., Working Woman, Success, Money, Venture, Business Week, Entrepreneur, In Business, The Chicago Tribune, The New York Times, The Boston Globe, Los Angeles Times*, and elsewhere.

He has authored and co-authored several books, including *New Venture Creation* (Richard D. Irwin, 1985), *The Encyclopedia of Small Business Resources* (Harper & Row, 1984), *The Insider's Guide to Small Business Resources* (Doubleday, 1982), *A Region's Struggling Savior* (SBA, 1980), and has co-edited three years of *Frontiers in Entrepreneurship Research* (Babson College, 1983, 1984 and 1985). His speaking and consulting assignments have included travels throughout the U.S. and Austria, Australia, Canada, Philippines, U.K., Scandanavia, Spain and elsewhere.

He is a graduate of Colgate University and received his MBA and doctorate from Harvard Business School.

Acknowledgements

There are many contributors to the ideas behind this book from whom I have drawn intellectual capital, and have received support and encouragement as well as inspiration. To list them all might well comprise a chapter by itself. Short of that, I wish to express special thanks to those who have been so helpful in recent years. First, my colleagues at Babson College and Harvard Business School who have been a constant source of encouragement, inspiration and friendship: Bill Bygrave, Alan Cohen, Neil Churchill, Jeff Ellis, Ned Goodhue, Dan Muzyka, Bob Reiser, Natalie Taylor, Bill Wetzel, Mel Copen, Bill Dill, J. B. Kassarjian, Tom Moore, and Gordon Prichett. Then our Price-Babson College Fellows: Stan Rich, Chuck Schmidt, Randy Wise, and especially Les Charm for his generous giving of time, entrepreneurial energy and resources to Babson. And all of the inductees into Babson's Academy of Distinguished Entrepreneurs, who have shared their entrepreneurial lives with us and have contributed so much to the legend and legacy of entrepreneurship at Babson College.

My dear friend and colleague, Professor Howard H. Stevenson, first Sarofim-Rock Professor at the Harvard Business School, stands alone for his support and generous sharing of his "world-class" intellectual capital and extraordinary wit. Howard, more than anyone else, has caused the academic community to focus on the role of opportunity in the entrepreneurial process.

Others who have been instrumental in furthering the entrepreneurial management mission and who have been supportive include Ron Fox; Bill Fruhan; Rosabeth Moss Kanter, first Class of 1960 Professor; Paul Lawrence; Marty Marshall; Dean John McArthur; Tom Piper; Mike Roberts; Bill Sahlman; and the Class of 1954.

Outside Babson and Harvard, several key people have given more to this effort than they shall ever know. Paul J. Tobin, president of Cellular One, Boston and the Boston Communications Group, has been a model entrepreneur and entrepreneurial manager in pioneering the car phone industry in America, along with the superb team at Cell One (Bob, Jean and Kim). I learn new lessons on entrepreneurial creativity and the nose for an opportunity each time I work with P.J. and see him and the team in action.

A special thanks is due Alexander L. M. Dingee, Jr., founder and president of Venture Founders Corporation, Lexington, Massachusetts, for his contributions to much of the material in chapters 13 through 17. His original work has been revised and additions made to it, but the numerous real-life examples and many of the lessons are derived from his experience as an entrepreneur.

Several other entrepreneurs and venture capitalists have been both sources of encouragement and my educators: Brion Applegate, Gordon Baty, Karl Baumgartner, Bill Egan, Joe Frye, Dave Gumpert, Doug Kahn, Paul Kelley, Earl Linehan, Jack Peterson, Len Smollen, John Van Slyke and The Fabb. A special thanks to my colleagues at Bridge Capital: Don Remey, Bart Goodwin, Hoyt Goodrich, Bill Spencer and Geoff Wadsworth, and advisors Craig Foley, Bill Foxley and Dick Johnson.

Harold Price, founder and benefactor, and Gloria Appel and the late Edwin M. Appel, of the Price Institute, have been staunch and unwavering champions of entrepreneurship at Babson College and across America. Their generous, pioneering support of the Price-Babson Fellows Program has made a major contribution toward cloning entrepreneurial minds—in both faculty and students—at colleges and universities worldwide. They have exceeded their prevoiously extraordinary generosity by making a $500 million challenge grant to Babson's Center for Entrepreneurial Studies to help us continue the mission and our work.

Hal Seigle, retired Chairman of The Sunmark Companies, St. Louis, and now a professional director and advisor to growing companies, has taught me a great deal about the difference between working hard and working smart, and in appreciating the difference between an idea and an opportunity. Watching him do both, always with a lot of class and integrity, has been a post-graduate course by itself.

My colleagues at Ernst & Young's national office in the Privately Owned Emerging Business group have opened my eyes to a whole new perspective of how it is possible for a Big Eight firm to be very entrepreneurial in seeking out new business opportunities and building their own business. They include Herb Braun, Gary Dando, Bill Casey, and Bruce Mantia (all in Cleveland), partners Ron Diegelman (Baltimore), Gayle Goodman (San Francisco), Dick Haddrill (Atlanta), Carl Mayhall (Dallas), Dick Nigon (Minneapolis), Ralph Sabin (Newport Beach), and Dale Sander (San Diego). They and Hy Shweil (Stamford) and members of the POEB Task Force have all worked with me to build a culture, a strategy and the know-how for providing value-added service opportunities as General Business Advisors to privately owned and emerging businesses.

A great debt of appreciation is perpetually due to all my former students from whom I learn with each encounter, and marvel both at their accomplishments and how little damage I imparted! Especially, Peter Altman, Avrum Belzar, Jeff Brown, Everett Dowling, Brian Dwyer, Joe Harris, Carl Hedberg, Greg Hunter, Jody Kosinski, Frank Mosvold, Greg Murphy, Steve Orne, Gerry Peterson, Steve Richards, Jim Turner and Marc Wallace, to name a few.

Finally, a special thanks is due Robert Runck, president of Brick House Publishing, whose unique entrepreneurial nose for opportunity was instrumental in making these three books possible. His creative approach to publishing ventures, and his excellent editorial wisdom and talent, is evident throughout the three books in this series. Without his energy, effort and contributions the books would never have been written. He is also living proof why smaller, entrepreneurial publishers can succeed in the land of the giants.

New Business Opportunities

1

What is an Idea?

Nothing is more dangerous than an idea, when it's the only one we have.
—Alain Emile Chartier

The Great Mousetrap Fallacy

Perhaps no one has done a greater disservice to generations of would-be entrepreneurs than Ralph Waldo Emerson, with his famous line, "If a man can make a better mousetrap than his neighbor, though he builds his house in the woods the world will make a beaten path to his door."

Who knows how many tens of thousands of potential entrepreneurs have been sidetracked, even ruined, by taking Emerson's advice to heart, by assuming that the core of a successful new enterprise is a novel idea or an invention. Indeed, success is apparently guaranteed if you can just come up with a new idea. And in today's rapidly changing world, if the idea has anything to do with technology, it is a cinch—or so it would seem.

The truth is that ideas, by themselves, are inert, and for all practical purposes, worthless. Take, for instance, the belief that someone who can obtain a patent for an idea or invention is bound to build a successful business from it. What is a patent really worth? Consider the following illustration.

At a leading New England engineering school, students are asked to search through issues of the Patent Gazette from ten years ago and select the ten patented ideas they believe are most promising for starting a new business. They are then asked to trace down the inventor and determine how much money was made on their "good ideas." The results are startling. Even with the advantage of hindsight and selectivity, less than one-tenth of one percent of the patented "good ideas" have resulted in financial gain for the inventor.

Why is this so? The lesson learned by successful entrepreneurs and venture capital investors is that there is an enormous difference between an idea—and an opportunity that leads to a successful venture. Inventors invent. They seek new ways and new ideas. Entrepreneurs are driven by business opportunity, anchored in customer needs, a favorable situation, competitive advantage, and timing—all of which adds up to one conclusion: "We can seize the opportunity, and now is the time."

In short, a sound product or idea is a necessary but not sufficient condition for launching, building and eventually harvesting a new venture. The entrepreneur is the catalyst who sees how and when an idea can be converted to a successful venture.

No idea or product has ever, by itself, started or run a company, or taken it public. A high-quality management team drives the process. Having a top-notch idea or innovation, and a first-rate entrepreneurial team, is the best of all worlds. But this doesn't happen very often. The dean of American venture capital, General Georges Doriot, is often quoted for his insistence that he preferred a Grade A entrepreneurial team with a Grade B idea to a Grade B team with a Grade A idea.[1]

Ideas Are a Dime a Dozen

Just listen, and look around. What is the flow of ideas for new products and services? How many have you heard of in the past week? How many can you write down in the next five minutes? In a half hour hundreds of ideas for products and services can be listed. Narrowing those lists to a few good opportunities is vastly more demanding.

The flow of ideas is really quite phenomenal. Many venture capital firms, for instance, during the investing boom of the 1980s, received two hundred or more proposals and business plans every month. Typically, only one to three percent of them actually received financing.

1. General Doriot founded American Research and Development Corporation in 1946 in Boston, the first institutional U.S. venture capital firm. AR&D put venture capital on the map by investing about $70,000 in 1957 in four young MIT engineers with an idea for a new computer. This investment grew to about $350 million—as shares in Digital Equipment Corporation, today America's second largest computer firm.

Having the best technology or idea does not make the critical difference in success. Numerous examples can be cited, but consider these:

UNIVAC (Sperry-Rand) had the early elegance and technology lead over IBM in computers, but was never able to seize the emerging, significant opportunities in the computer industry.

When one of today's leading minicomputer firms, Data General, was formed in 1968, there were several other new minicomputer ventures started about the same period. Several of these actually had a better idea in the form of more advanced technology. Yet DG's lead entrepreneur and his team, all under thirty years of age when they started the company, had an entrepreneurial flair and market focus.[2]

In 1969, the then fledgling Cullinet, Inc., raised $500,000 in a hot new-issues stock market. Two years later the firm had spent this capital, and, according to its founder, John Cullinane, still had a payroll of $8,500 to meet. How was the money spent? Through "programmer anarchy," according to Mr. Cullinane. He turned the company around by firing the programmers. "Happiness," Cullinane has said, "is a satisfied customer."

By 1977 Cullinane had developed customer-anchored software products, and a plan for growth that led to a substantial venture-capital investment at a time when venture capital was tight.

In 1981 Adam Osborne developed and marketed the first portable microcomputer. By 1985 Osborne Computer was bankrupt, having been displaced by another start-up firm, COMPAQ.

The pattern of new ventures in microcomputer software provides numerous other examples of the "better idea without better management" that went nowhere. Take, for instance, Visicalc, the first spreadsheet software program for microcomputers, and Lotus 1-2-3, the Visicalc clone that has become the national champ of software products.

2. Tracy Kidder, *The Soul of a New Machine*, Little Brown, 1981. An excellent book, well worth reading.

Visicalc had the market all to itself at first, but was not marketed effectively and not kept up to date in a timely way. Lotus 1-2-3 was the first software product that received a major national marketing effort, setting the pace for the industry. Visicalc has disappeared, and Lotus is a major player in software.

As a result of Lotus raising the ante, new software products today are unlikely to gain a significant share of market without $5 million or more of capital to gain the necessary attention and distribution in this tumultuous marketplace. Having a top-notch new product is very important, but it is only one ingredient of success.

Inventors Are Not Entrepreneurs

Somehow the distinction between the inventive genius of a Thomas Edison and the creative entrepreneur is often confused. Edison was a remarkable person, but what is less well known is that he earned practically nothing from his many inventions. Many aspiring entrepreneurs, operating unwittingly on the Edison role model, are bound to become frustrated and disenchanted when their imaginative ideas earn nothing more than admiration from peers.

Particularly susceptible to the "better mousetrap" fallacy are the aspiring but inexperienced entrepreneurs who possesses an engineering, technical, academic or research and development background. Many of them have been sheltered from the tough, competitive realities of the business world. One consequence of this is to underestimate, if not seriously downgrade, the importance of what it takes to make a business succeed.

Another contribution to the fallacy are shallow and stereotyped accounts of how ventures such as Xerox, IBM, and Polaroid made their founders wealthy. Such oversimplified versions of what happened make it seem to have been easy or inevitable.

Another source of this "mousetrap myopia" lies in the technical and scientific orientation to "do it better than ever." A good illustration of this is a Canadian entrepreneur who manufactured truck seats. He related how he and his brother, an engineer, started a business:

"My brother developed a new seat for trucks. It was a definite improvement, so we started a business to manufacture and sell them. I knew we could profitably sell the seat he had designed, and we did so. Then we needed more manufacturing capacity—we could sell all we could make. But my brother wasn't as interested in that. He had several ideas on how to improve the seat, as well as design some new ones.

"If I had listened to him we probably would be a small custom shop today, or out of business. Instead, we concentrated on making seats that would sell at a profit, rather than just making a better seat. Our company has several million dollars of sales today and is profitable."

The stress on perfection—on making the best widget ever and improving it in any small way possible—places undue emphasis on the product. This emphasis usually excludes consideration of the marketplace: the wants and needs of the person expected to buy it. A good opportunity is a product or service which creates or adds value for its buyers or end users.

Another factor contributing to mousetrap myopia is intense ego involvement with a new widget which tends to cloud business considerations: realistic assessment of market potential, getting the product ready for the market, gaining customer acceptance, and assessing the real value of the invention, potentially an obstacle in attracting investors and a management team. Such an intense level of psychological involvement is necessary for creating a new business, but a fatal flaw is the *narrowness* of its focus. Successful entrepreneurs who build a substantial business possess the intense commitment—but focus it on building the business, not just on the idea or product.

The Experience Factor

What is it that enables entrepreneurs to spot an idea for which there is a good venture opportunity? More than anything else, it is experience. They've been there. They have a sense of what will work and what will stumble. And relevant experience can be quite independent of age—contrast youthful Steve Jobs, Apple Computer founder, with the late Ray Kroc, who founded McDonald's when he was over fifty.

There is a common denominator among successful start-ups: In 95% of these cases the founders launch a new venture in the same marketplace, technology and industry where they acquired the bulk of their own experience. They operate in familiar territory. The more sophisticated the technology or marketing of the venture is, the more important this prior experience seems to be.

That does not mean that you cannot launch and grow a successful venture in a business with which you have no experience. It is simply that one way to get the odds in favor of recognizing a good opportunity buried in a new idea is to get some relevant experience first. It can take ten or even fifteen years or more to accumulate the experience, know-how and recognition of patterns which culminate in the creative ability to recognize an opportunity clearly that may only be a blur to others.

Pattern Recognition

Successful entrepreneurs are able to recognize a pattern while it is still taking shape. They recognize that an idea has possibilities for "ringing a customer's bell." These entrepreneurs do not require large, statistically reliable samples and control groups in order to conclude there is an opportunity. To illustrate:

Vincent Keenan spent fifteen years after his graduation from college working with leading financial institutions. His last job before launching his own firm was as vice president of the tax-shelter group for Dean, Witter, Inc. He thus gained extensive experience in managing a large office and dealing with upper-income customers.

To meet their needs for tax advice and planning, he orchestrated the development of in-house software to keep track of their accounts and assets, and to provide analysis of various scenarios. He knew little, in a technical sense, about computers and computer programming at the time. He used them simply as tools to meet customer needs.

With the advent of the microcomputer he saw a pattern that led to his venture: a link between the idea (personal financial planning software) and the needs of his customers. He was convinced a new business could be built around the idea. It was a good opportunity, in his view, since he was intimately familiar with both customer needs and the lack of serious competition. In the early 1980s his firm and software, THE FINANCIER, gained recognition as an early leader in this rapidly developing industry.

Howard Head describes how he decided he could develop the oversized Prince tennis racket into a successful venture. "I saw the pattern again that had worked at Head Ski," he said. "I had proven to myself before that you can take different technology and know-how and apply it to a solution in a new area."

Head had been an aeronautical design engineer working with new light-metal alloys to build more efficient airfoils during World War II. Although he had limited skiing experience, he concluded that if he could make a metal ski there would be a significant market, due to the limitations of wooden skis.

He later tried tennis with a conventional racket, and realized there was a real need for ball control among novice players. He then set about learning enough about the physics of tennis rackets and surfaces to develop the oversized Prince racket. The company has become a major factor in the industry, and the second very successful "harvest" for Mr. Head.

A lesser known young entrepreneur parlayed experience as a loan officer with a large New York City bank into a job with a manufacturer of mobile and modular homes in Texas. This enabled him, over a three-year period, to learn the business and to understand the market opportunity. He opened one sales location in a growing suburb about twenty-five miles from one of the booming larger cities. The business provided him with a decent living, but he looked for ways to expand.

By studying his competitors, and conducting an analysis of how customers actually went about purchasing a new modular home, he spotted a pattern that meant opportunity. Customers usually shopped at three different locations, each with different models and price ranges, before making a purchase decision. So what did he do? Since his market analysis showed room in his city for three, maybe four such businesses, he initiated an insightful strategy.

He opened two additional lots, each with a different name, and with different but complementary lines. Within two years, despite record high interest rates, his business had nearly tripled to $17 million in annual sales, and his only competitor was planning to move.

This is an excellent example of how the best ideas invariably deal with ways to provide the customers with what they want, rather than with the product itself.

Note that each of these entrepreneurs created new businesses by linking knowledge in one field or marketplace with know-how in another technical or business and marketing area: financial planning needs with microcomputer technology; buying habits with a marketing strategy; new metal fabrication techniques with skill in downhill skiing. Such cross-associating and creative linking is a product of experience and the ability to see how patterns in one area can also work in another.

Trial and Error Works

The new business that simply bursts from a flash of brilliance is rare. They do happen, but they are exceptions. What is usually necessary is a series of trial and error iterations, or repetitions, until the crude idea fits what the customer is willing to pay for, and provides high gross margins as well. In technology ventures, these iterations often occur during the development and refinement of the prototype. The main issue to be resolved is: will it work? After all, Howard Head made a total of forty different metal skis until he finally got one to work consistently.

The hard realities for entrepreneurs are that there are so many variables, and so many constantly changing situations, that refining an idea into an opportunity necessitates a lot of trial and error experimentation. To make matters worse, there is not much theory to guide those experiments. Thus, the role of relevant experience becomes paramount once again.

There are many examples of the first product or service being only a point of departure for an emerging company. With surprising frequency a major business is built on totally different products or applications than were originally envisioned. Consider these examples:

F. Leland Strange, the founder and President of QUADRAM, maker of graphics, communications and other boards for microcomputers, told the story of how he developed his marketing idea into a company with $100 million in sales in three years. Mr. Strange was a marketing professor. When asked whether he had *developed a business plan to launch his own company, he responded, "Of course." The company even hit its projected revenues for the first two years. The only thing was, he noted, it was based upon different products than those defined in the original plan!*

Polaroid Corporation, the camera company, was founded on the principle of polarizing light waves, a discovery by Dr. Edwin Land which he patented. It was reasoned that such a product would have the compelling safety feature of eliminating head-on nighttime collisions due to blinding by oncoming lights.

Conceivably, such polarized lamps could be installed in every vehicle manufactured. The company grew to its present billion dollar plus size through a quite different application of the original technology—instant photography—which was not one of its original ideas.

IBM, the world's largest mainframe computer manufacturer, and now the market leader in personal computers as well, began in the wire and cable business, and later expanded to time clocks. Sales in the 1920s were only a few million dollars a year. The computer business emerged much later.

How important is the original idea to the development of a significant business? By itself, not much at all. With hindsight, it looks critical. But it is likely to endure and become a business only if anchored in the need of the customer, with real benefits and value added. Ideas for new ventures are important, of course, but they tend to be overrated, usually at the expense of other vital driving forces.

Central to the entrepreneurial process is the creative linking or cross-fertilizing of two or more in-depth chunks of experience, know-how and contacts. Such creativity is associative—connecting apparently unrelated things—rather than linear, or simply additive. Entrepreneurial opportunities come of seeing how one plus one can equal three or more.

The process is inductive, one of intelligent trial and error in finding ideas for products and services with significant market opportunity and potential, and in revising, retesting and further reapplying these ideas until a profitable match-up with the customer is achieved. This process is fundamentally a human one: having the capacity to recognize patterns, and to seize and execute opportunities.

2

Enhancing Creativity

Can anyone seriously question the potential value of creative thinking in linking a product or service to the customer, devising innovative marketing and sales approaches, or solving troublesome problems? Creativity of all kinds plays a central role in entrepreneuring. Can creativity be enhanced? Fortunately, the answer is "yes."

The Nature of Creative Thinking

Most people can spot creativity and the creative acts of others. School children and college students all seem to know who, among their peers, are the ones with a creative flair. What may not be so well known, however, is that creativity actually peaks during, usually, the first grade. A lot of things account for that. For one thing, life tends to become increasingly structured and defined by others through childhood and adolescence. For another, most of education beyond grade school stresses logical reasoning and sequential thinking. Finally, social pressure can tame creativity. The entrepreneurial mind, in contrast, tends to be creative and nonrational, stimulated by the chaotic and unknown.

The good news is that creative thinking can be enhanced. You don't have to be a genius or an artist to be a creative thinker. Not as easy as it sounds, but some experts believe looking at old problems in new ways, from different angles, can be learned by most people with the willingness and patience to apply themselves.

Take, for instance, a group called Synectics, one of the first organizations to investigate systematically—in the early 1950s—the process of creative thinking and how to harness it.[1]

The term "synectics" means the joining together of different or apparently irrelevant parts. The Synectics Group applied their principles to integrating diverse individuals into problem-defining and problem-solving groups.

2. See William J. J. Gordon, *Synectics*, 1961.

The theories underlying this approach to developing creativity were threefold:

• Creative efficiency in people can be markedly increased if they understand the psychological process by which they operate.

• In the creative process, the emotional component is more important than the intellectual, the irrational more important than the rational.

• It is the emotional, irrational elements which must be understood in order to increase the probability of success in a problem-solving situation.

The Synectics approach was novel. It began with the selection of groups to attend the training sessions, involved learning the methods and techniques based on the above principles, and concluded with efforts to integrate into the client's business or organization the solutions generated by the groups.

The methods do unlock the thinking process, and they seem to yield imaginative solutions. Take, for instance, a typical problem assigned to a group: design a vertical anchor for boats. To detach thinking from the conventional and rational, novel techniques were introduced. One involved getting a volunteer from the group to actually lie on the floor, eyes closed, and imagine that *he* was the anchor. With some guidance from the trainer, the group urged the "human anchor" to tell them what it felt like to be an anchor on the bottom of the sea!

They then pushed and tugged at the "anchor" to elicit further imaginative reactions. The uninhibited process of physically and mentally attempting to feel and think what it is like to be some kind of device that will secure a boat vertically elicited both laughter and imagination.

Amid the hilarity that accompanied such sessions, a genuine respect for the techniques emerged. Group members conceded that they came up with ideas and creative solutions during these freewheeling, uninhibited voyages into collective creativity that they have never experienced before.

Left Brain—Right Brain

Since the 1950s a good deal more has been learned about the working of the human brain. Today, there is general agreement that the two sides of the brain process information in quite different ways. The left side performs the rational, logical functions, while the right side operates the intuitive and non-rational modes of thought. Of course, we use both sides, shifting from one mode to the other.

Here is an exercise that appears in a book by an art teacher who developed a method of teaching drawing based upon left-side, right-side insights into the brain's functioning.[2]

In the exercise, it is important to experience the shift from one mode to the other—the shift from the ordinary verbal, analytic state to the spatial, nonverbal state. By setting up the conditions for this mental shift and experiencing the slightly different feeling it produces, a person can recognize and foster at will this state of being able to draw.

Vases and Faces: An Exercise for the Double Brain

The exercises that follow are specifically designed to help you shift from your dominant left-hemisphere mode to your subdominant R-mode. I could go on describing the process over and over in words, but only *you* can experience for yourself this cognitive shift, this slight change in subjective state. As Fats Waller once said, "If you gotta ask what jazz is, you ain't never gonna know." So it is with the R-mode state: you must experience the L- to R-mode shift, observe the R-mode state, and in this way come to know it.

You have probably seen the perceptual-illusion drawing of the vase and faces. Looked at one way, the drawing appears to be two faces seen in profile. Then, as you are looking at it, the drawing seems to change and become a vase. One version of the drawing is shown in Figure a.

Before you begin: First, read all the directions for the exercise.

1. Draw a profile of a person's head on the *left* side of the paper, facing toward the center. (If you are left-handed, draw the profile on the right side, facing toward the center.) Examples are shown of both the right-handed and left-handed drawings (Figures b and c).

2. Betty Edwards, *Drawing on the Right Side of the Brain*, 1979, Houghton-Mifflin/ J. B. Tarcher, Inc.

Make up your own version of the profile if you wish. It seems to help if this profile comes from your own memorized, stored *symbols* for a human profile.

2. Next, draw horizontal lines at the top and bottom of your profile, forming top and bottom of the vase (Figures b and c).

Figure a

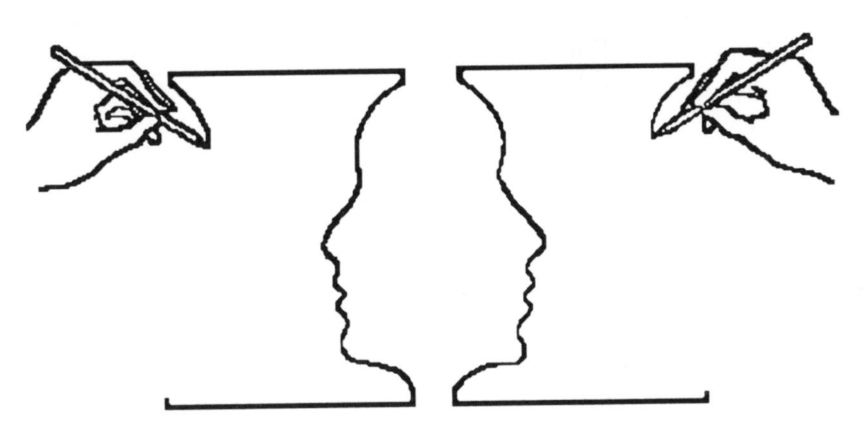

Figure b (for left-handers) Figure c (for right-handers)

3. Now go back over your drawing of the first profile with your pencil. As the pencil moves over the features, *name them to yourself*: forehead, nose, upper lip, chin, neck. Repeat this step at least once. This is an L-mode task: naming symbolic shapes.

4. Next, starting at the top, draw the profile in *reverse*. By doing this, you will *complete the vase*. The second profile should be a reversal of the first in order for the vase to by symmetrical. (Look once more at the example in Figure a.) Watch for the faint signals from your brain that you are shifting modes of information processing. You may experience a sense of mental conflict at some point in the drawing of the *second* profile. Observe this. And observe *how you solve the problem*. You will find that you are doing the second profile *differently. This is right-hemisphere-mode drawing.*

Before you read further, do the drawing.

After you finish: Now that you have completed the vases-faces drawing, think back on how you did it. The first profile was probably rather rapidly drawn and then, as you were instructed, redrawn while verbalizing the names of the parts as you went back over the features.

This is a left-hemisphere mode of processing: *drawing symbolic shapes from memory and naming them*.

In drawing the second profile (that is, the profile that completes the vase), you may have experienced some confusion or conflict, as I mentioned. To continue the drawing, you had to find a different way, some different process. You probably lost the sense of drawing a profile and found yourself *scanning* back and forth in the space between the profiles, estimating angles, curves, inward-curving and outward-curving shapes, and lengths of line *in relation to* the opposite shapes, which now become *unnamed and unnamable*. Putting it another way, you made constant adjustments in the line you were drawing by checking *where you were* and *where you were going*, by scanning the space between the first profile and your copy in reverse.

In short, you began by drawing a symbol for a *face*; you concluded by drawing a *line*—the same result, but achieved by an entirely different process.

Using the research from the medical profession as well as her own observations, Edwards has drawn up a list of left-mode and right-mode characteristics:

L-Mode

Verbal: Using words to name, describe, define.

Analytic: Figuring things out step-by-step and part-by-part.

Symbolic: Using a symbol to *stand for* something. For example, the sign + stands for the process of addition.

Abstract: Taking out a small bit of information and using it to represent the whole thing.

Temporal: Keeping track of time, sequencing one thing after another: Doing first things first, second things second, etc.

Rational: Drawing conclusions based on *reason* and *facts*.

Digital: Using numbers as in counting.

Logical: Drawing conclusions based on logic: one thing following another in logical order—for example, a mathematical theorem or a well-stated argument.

Linear: Thinking in terms of linked ideas, one thought directly following another, often leading to a convergent conclusion.

R-mode

Nonverbal: Awareness of things, but minimal connection with words.

Synthetic: Putting things together to form wholes.

Concrete: Relating to things as they are at the present moment.

Analogic: Seeing likenesses between things; understanding metaphoric relationships.

Nontemporal: Without a sense of time.

Nonrational: Not requiring a basis in reason or facts; willingness to suspend judgment.

Spatial: Seeing where things are in relation to other things, and how parts go together to form a whole.

Intuitive: Making leaps of insight, often based on incomplete patterns, hunches, feelings, or visual images.

Holistic: Seeing whole things all at once; perceiving overall patterns and structures, often leading to divergent conclusions.

Research indicates, and you yourself have seen, that you can be in either one mode or the other, but not in both modes simultaneously.

Therefore, the trick is to tell your left-mode to shut up when you want to approach a problem differently—in a non-temporal, non-verbal way. It works!

A further exercise in the Edwards book is an interesting one for anyone who is convinced that he or she "can't draw a straight line." It involves copying a line drawing done by the famous artist Picasso of the famous musician Igor Stravinsky—but the image is shown upside down.

Within a very few minutes, you will have forgotten what you are copying and becoming interested only in how the lines fit together. When you have finished you probably will be unaware of how much time has elapsed. Best of all, when you turn your drawing right side up, it will look uncannily like Picasso's. How could you have done it? The answer appears to rest in the right side of your brain. Not only is creative thinking very useful, it is also fun.

The author of another book on creativity sums up this attitude: "I like to think of creative thinking as the 'sex of our mental lives.' Ideas, like organisms, have a life cycle. They are born, they develop, they reach maturity, and they die. So we need a way to generate new ideas. Creative thinking is that means, and like its biological counterpart, it is also pleasurable."[3]

As you might surmise from the book's title, *A Whack on the Side of the Head*, the author takes a lighthearted, but eminently workable, approach to the problem. He has compiled a list of 10 "mental locks" which interfere with creative thinking and suggests ways to unlock them. As you go through the iterations of developing and refining an idea for a product or service that will capture customer enthusiasm, consider his list of creativity blockers:

The Right Answer	To Err is Wrong
That's Not Logical	Play is Frivolous
Follow the Rules	That's Not My Area
Be Practical	Don't Be Foolish
Avoid Ambiguity	I'm Not Creative

3. Roger von Oech, *A Whack on the Side of the Head*, 1983, Warner Books.

As is evident, these "mental locks" are the offspring of left-brain thinking. The obvious implication for an entrepreneur is: What if you tend to be more left-brain than right-brain in your thinking? You may have quite extraordinary logical and rational powers, and develop some wonderful technical solutions to a problem, but never really capture the customer's enthusiasm. Now what?

The Concept of Team Creativity

Individual creativity is stunning when you witness it. But truly creative geniuses are few and far between. What is more, in our rapidly moving, fragile world, customers and the marketplace do not stand still long enough for a creative genius to surface in your venture, if that person is not you. Fortunately, you do not have to rely on a genius-inspired breakthrough to do well.

What is continually impressive is the creativity of a team. To watch group creativity in action, try the following problem. First, pull together two to four teams of three to five persons each. Have at least five individuals work alone on the problem. Record the various solutions and how much time was required (it should not take more than 15–20 minutes).

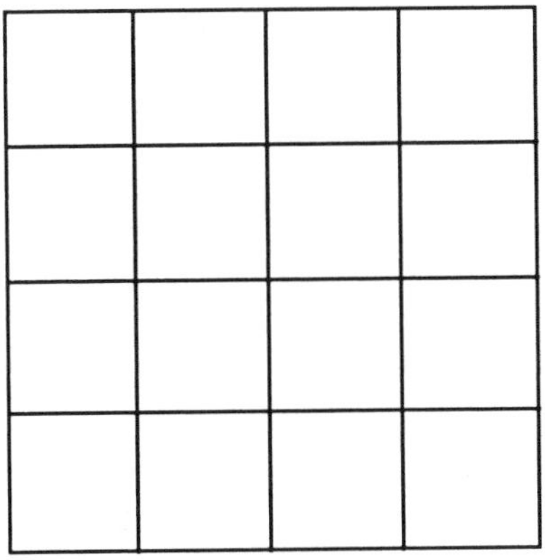

The figure shown here is a square box on a single, flat plane. Assume that all of the angles are right angles, and the sides are of equal length. The task is to count up the *total number of squares* you see in the figure. (An explanation appears at the end of the chapter.)

Implications for Entrepreneurs

If there is a myth about entrepreneurs and creativity, it is the "fallacy of the one big brain." You do not have to have all of the creativity yourself to build a successful company. But unless there is some strong creativity in your team, you have one strike against you to start.

One good example of the balanced team concept is a company founded by a business-college graduate with little technical training. He teamed up with a talented inventor/technologist. The entrepreneurial and business know-how of the founder complemented the creative and technical skills of the inventor. The results have been a rapidly growing multi-million dollar venture in the field of video-based surgical equipment.

In summary, research shows that creativity and intuition rest in the right side of the brain, and can be nurtured, some say even learned. Logic and rationality, the domain of the left-brain, often clash with the free-wheeling, intuitive nature of the entrepreneur, and lead to many paradoxes. Moreover, teams can generate creativity that may not exist in a single individual.

(Solution to creative squares: 16 single squares; 1 large square; 4 corners, 2X2; 4 corners, 3X3; 4 middle, 2X2; 1 center, 2X2 = 30 squares in total.)

3

Sources of New Business Ideas

Chances are you already have plenty of ideas that might lead to a new venture. The real challenge, of course, is to identify those ideas that are serious opportunities. What if you do not have any particular idea for starting a company? Where can you look?

New venture ideas come from a multitude of sources, contacts and experiences. In his book *New Venture Strategies*, Karl Vesper suggests a wide variety of potential sources beyond work experience, including hobbies, social encounters, self-employment, moonlighting, and a deliberate search.[1]

Following is a summary of leading sources and information services. They are not meant to be all-inclusive, but as a guide to some general areas where ideas can be found.

Product-Licensing Information Services

One good way to obtain exposure to a large number of product ideas that are available from universities, corporations, and independent investors is to subscribe to one of the services that periodically publish data on products available for licensing.

There are a variety of these services, and they cover the United States as well as foreign countries. The products range from simple toys and gadgets to sophisticated high-technology products. Some services do a better job of screening than others do, and the amount of product information provided can range from a patent abstract to a one-page description with pictures and proposed licensing terms.

To obtain additional information, a subscriber must contact the potential licensor. Some services publish the licensor's name and address as part of their product information.

1. Karl H. Vesper, *New Venture Strategies*, 1980, Prentice-Hall, ch 5.

Others code their licensor listings, require that initial inquiries go through them, and charge an inquiry fee.

American Bulletin of International Technology Transfer
554 Wilshire Boulevard
Los Angeles, California 90036
Annual subscriptions are $120 for this bimonthly publication and there is a $5-per-item inquiry charge to subscribers. This service provides listings of product and service opportunities sought or offered for licensing by organizations throughout the world.

General Electric Selected Business Ventures (SBV)
Business Growth Services
One River Road
Schenectady, New York 12345
Originally a publication for marketing selected GE products, this program now identifies new product opportunities available from a number of U.S. and foreign organizations. Products are classified in one or more of eight different categories (e.g., Electronic and Electromechanical; Consumer Products; Measuring, Testing, and Controls; Medical; etc.)

Each month subscribers receive announcements of selected products available for licensing in the categories to which they subscribe. An annual subscription to any one product category is $175, with decreasing prices for additional categories. An annual subscription to all eight categories is $725. Each product is described on a file card that also contains the name and address of the prospective licensor and sometimes the proposed licensing terms.

Technology Mart
Thomas Publishing Company
250 West 34th Street
New York, New York 10001
Annual subscriptions are $72 for this bimonthly publication, and there is no inquiry fee for subscribers. Technology Mart publishes data on products and processes available for international license, divestiture

opportunities involving product lines or even corporate divisions, and U.S. government technology available for license.

Patent Licensing Gazette

Techni Research Associates, Inc.
Professional Center Building
Willow Grove, Pennsylvania 19090

Annual subscriptions are $32 for this bimonthly publication. It provides abstracts of screened patents available for licensing from domestic and foreign organizations. Names and addresses of the prospective licensors are given.

National Technical Information Service (NTIS)

U.S. Department of Commerce
P.O. Box 1533
Springfield, Virginia 22151

An annual subscription of $165 provides NTIS weekly abstracts of government inventions available for licensing. This publication covers government inventions believed to have commercial potential that are available from all major government agencies (e.g., NASA, AEC, HEW, etc.). Descriptions of inventions tend to be very brief and technical. Additional information is available in patent applications.

Although government licenses are generally granted on a nonexclusive basis, some agencies can grant exclusive licenses when this is necessary to attract risk capital to commercialize government technology.

International New Product Newsletter

Box 191
Back Bay Annex
Boston, Massachusetts 02116

Annual subscription is $75 for this semi-monthly publication that describes products and processes available for license, primarily from sources outside of the United States. Products and processes included are those considered to have reasonably immediate commercial potential.

Dr. Dvorkovitz and Associates
P.O. Box 1748
Ormond Beach, Florida 32074

Dvorkovitz has the world's largest computerized file of products, processes, and technology available for license. About 8,000 items are listed in his data bank, replenished and updated by 20 representatives in contact with innovating groups in over 50 countries. Data on available products are supplied weekly as computer printouts or through an interactive display terminal at the subscriber's location that communicates with a central computer.

Dvorkovitz's principal customers are major corporations. Dvorkovitz classifies his technology available for license into 99 categories, and the annual price for a subscriber to monitor any one category is $2,000. The price per additional category is somewhat discounted and product information in all categories is $32,500 per year, including a computer terminal to query the data bank.

Patent Brokers

Patent brokers specialize in marketing patents that are owned by individual inventors, corporations, universities, or other research organizations to companies or entrepreneurs seeking new, commercially viable products. Some brokers specialize in international product licensing.

Occasionally a patent broker will purchase an invention and then try to resell it to a manufacturer. More often a patent broker acts as an agent for an organization or individual inventor seeking to sell a patent or invention. In this situation, the broker is compensated by a commission or flat fee (from the buyer or seller or both), or by a percentage of royalties. In some cases, from a young, cash-short company acquiring rights to a patent, the broker may take some or all of his fee as stock.

Over the years, the patent broker's image has occasionally been tarnished by a few unscrupulous brokers taking advantage of inventors by charging them a fee and then doing little to sell their inventions. However, inventions sold by reputable brokers have resulted in significant new products. Notable among these was Bausch and Lomb's acquisition, through National Patent Development Corporation, of the U.S. rights to Hydron (developed in Czechoslovakia), a material used in contact lenses.

The following are reputable patent brokers.

MGA Technology, Inc.
Wrigley Building
400 North Michigan Avenue
Chicago, Illinois 60611

New Product Development Services, Inc.
900 State Line Road
P.O. Box 8424
Kansas City, Missouri 64114

University Patents
875 North Michigan Avenue
Chicago, Illinois 60611

Research Corporation
405 Lexington Avenue
New York, New York 10174

Pegasus International
625 Madison Avenue
New York, New York 10022

National Patent Development Corporation
375 Park Avenue
New York, New York 10022

Corporations

Almost all corporations engaged in research and development have developed ideas they have not exploited commercially, because the ideas do not fit existing product lines or marketing programs, or do not seem likely to attract a sufficiently large market to interest a large corporation.

A number of corporations now seek to license these kinds of inventions. Some corporations use patent brokers and/or product-licensing information services to sell their inventions, or try to sell their technology through their own patent marketing efforts. By contacting a corporation with a licensing program directly, an entrepreneur may avoid the costs of a product-licensing information service or a patent broker, but he will not be exposed to a full range of corporate licensing opportunities.

Among the major corporations known to have active internal patent marketing efforts are:

Gulf and Western Invention Development Corp.
1 Gulf and Western Plaza
New York, New York 10023

Kraft Corporation Research and Development
801 Waukegan Road
Glenview, Illinois 60025

Pillsbury Company Research and Development Laboratories
311 Second Street SE
Minneapolis, Minnesota 55414

Union Carbide Corporation
Nuclear Division
Oak Ridge, Tennessee 37830

RCA Corportion Domestic Licensing
1133 Avenue of the Americas
New York, New York 10036

TRW Corporation Patent and Technology Application Office
Systems Group
1 Space Park
Redondo, California

Lockheed Corporation Patent Licensing
Missile and Space Division
Sunnyvale, California

Not-for-Profit Research Institutes

There are nonprofit organizations that do research and development under contract to the government and private industry. These organizations also do some internally sponsored research and development to develop new products and processes that can be licensed to private corporations for further development, manufacturing, and marketing.

Perhaps the most famous example is Battelle Memorial Institute's participation in the development of Xerography and the subsequent license of the technology (for a stock interest!) to the Haloid Corporation, now Xerox Corp.

Some of the not-for-profit research institutes with active licensing programs are:

Battelle Memorial Institute
Columbus, Ohio
ITT Research Institute
Chicago, Illinois
Stanford Research Institute
Palo Alto, California
Southwest Research Institute
San Antonio, Texas

Universities

A number of universities active in research in the physical sciences seek to license inventions that result from this research. This is done directly by a university or through an associated foundation that administers its patent program. Among the universities that have active licensing programs are:

Massachusetts Institute of Technology
California Institute of Technology
via the California Research Foundation

(M.I.T. and CalTech publish periodic reports that contain abstracts of inventions they own that are available for licensing.)
University of Wisconsin via the Wisconsin Alumni Research Foundation
Iowa State University via the Iowa State University Research Foundation
Purdue University via the Purdue Research Foundation
University of California
University of Oregon, Innovation Center.

However, a number of very good ideas developed in universities never reach the patent offices. Another way to find technological opportunities at a university—particularly if you are there as a student or researcher—is to become familiar with the work of researchers in your areas of interest, to see if anything they are doing could form the basis of a business. They might even join you in such a venture.

A number of high-technology businesses in Boston were started this way. One example is a company that was started to manufacture an electro-optical hygrometer that was developed by an M.I.T. student in support of his research. This sort of laboratory contact can also be used to find product opportunities in the laboratories of medical schools.

Industry and Trade Contacts

If you have decided on the industry and market area in which you want to establish a venture, there are a number of contacts you can make and things you can do to seek product ideas for a venture in that industry.

Ideas from Customers. If you are clear enough about the type of product you want to make to be able to identify potential customers, you can meet with them and determine what their needs are and where existing products are deficient or inadequate. For example, if you wanted to enter the biomedical equipment business, discussions with doctors who are heads of medical services at leading hospitals (and potential customers) might lead to product ideas for your venture.

Ideas from Distributors and Wholesalers. Contact those people who distribute the kinds of products you might want to manufacture and sell, and seek their advice on new product requirements. Distributors and wholesalers can have an extensive knowledge of the strengths and weaknesses of existing products and the kinds of product improvements and new products that are needed by their customers.

Ideas from Competitors. Examine closely the products offered by those companies that might be your competitors. If a competitive product is in your area of interest, evaluate whether you can improve on an existing design and come up with a product that can sell against the competition.

Your product should not infringe on the patents of your competitor, but for many products, it is often easy to design around patent claims. Although it's nice to be the one to introduce a product, an imitator who moves quickly with a better product can often achieve a substantial market share.

One example in the recreational vehicle field is an improved version of an established trailer accessory which achieved sales in excess of $1 million in its introductory year, in spite of the limited experience of the management in that business.

Ideas from Trade Shows. Trade shows covering the industry you want to enter can be an excellent way to examine the products of many of your potential competitors, meet distributors and sales representatives, learn of product and market trends, and identify potential products for your venture.

Professional Contacts. Ideas can also be found by contacting business and professional people in your vicinity that come into contact with inventors seeking to license their patents or to start a business using them. Among the professionals that might be contacted are patent attorneys, accountants, commercial bankers, and venture capitalists.

Former Employers. A number of technology-based businesses have made use of technology and ideas developed by the entrepreneur in a previous employment. In many cases the development was done at research laboratories not interested in commercial exploitation of technology, and/or under a government contract that put the technology in the public domain.

In other cases, entrepreneurs developed ideas to improve products and sold the ideas to their former employers. Conversely, some employers were not interested, and sold or gave the rights to the entrepreneur to start his own company. Some companies will even help an entrepreneur set up a company in return for equity in it.

An entrepreneur who intends to use a product or service idea derived from former employment must be careful not to infringe on patents or trade secrets, nor violate noncompete terms of an employment contract. In such cases it is a good idea to consult an attorney before going too far with a venture idea.

Working as a Consultant

A method for obtaining ideas that has often been successful for technically trained entrepreneurs is to provide consulting and one-of-a-kind engineering designs for people in a field of interest to the entrepreneur who need this service. For example, if you wanted to establish a medical equipment company, try doing consulting and designing experimental equipment for medical researchers. Or, perhaps you can provide engineering consulting to physicists, biologists, or oceanographers needing special kinds of instrumentation. These kinds of activities often lead to prototypes that can be turned into products needed by a number of researchers.

Networking

The concept of networking has gained much attention in recent years. Developing an "old boy/girl network" of contacts is an important part of entrepreneuring. Such networks can be a stimulant and source of new ideas for businesses, as well as providing valuable contacts with people and resources. Much of this requires personal initiative on an informal basis. But increasingly, in entrepreneurial "hotbeds" around the country, organized networks are cropping up that can facilitate and accelerate the process of making contacts, and finding new business ideas.

The *American Electronics Association* offers a variety of seminars and trade meetings where the latest ideas and developments are shown.

American Women's Economic Development Corporation (AWED) in New York City has operated since 1976 as a means for networking and assisting female entrepreneurs (212-347-5195). There are national associations as well, including the *Association of Women Entrepreneurs* (402-474-2058), and the *National Association of Women Business Owners* (NAWBO), with chapters in several major cities (202-338-8966).

The UCLA Graduate Student Association has created the *Entrepreneur's Roundtable* to link practicing entrepreneurs with MBA students there. Contact Dean Al Osborne.

Wichita State University has initiated an *Association of Collegiate Entrepreneurs* (ACE), with chapters at colleges around the nation. The first annual gathering of ACE occurred at M.I.T. in April 1984. Attendees were stimulated and challenged by the student entrepreneurs they met there. Contact professor Fran Jabara.

The Boston area is a high density area of exceptional entrepreneurial activity. Several networking mechanisms have emerged in recent years. (With a little detective work, you can find similar organizations in your area of the country.)

Babson Entrepreneurial Exchange, an organization of area entrepreneurs, students and alumni of Babson College who meet several times a year to exchange ideas, make contacts, and to help each other with their entrepreneurial activities. These gatherings include developing leads for student internships, small workshops for trying out an idea or a business plan, and finding professional assistance. Call Professor William Bygrave at Babson (617-235-4567).

SBANE, the Smaller Business Association of New England, sponsors a monthly session whose sole purpose is to meet other entrepreneurs, exchange business cards and ideas (617-890-9070).

M.I.T. Enterprise Forum meets monthly to enable entrepreneurs to present their start-up or expansion plan to a large audience (often 100 or more), and a panel consisting of entrepreneurs, venture capitalists, and others. It is an excellent vehicle to learn about new technology ideas, and how technology-based entrepreneurs approach a new venture. Similar forums have recently been created in the Baltimore-Washington area and Los Angeles, with M.I.T. alumni and other groups. Contact Paul E. Johnson (616-253-8240).

The 128 Venture Group was launched to create a monthly interchange among entrepreneurs and innovators, management team prospects, and venture capitalists. Entrepreneurs at each meeting describe their business idea, managers tell of their relevant experience, and investors hope they can find their way into a profitable match-up. A group has also been launched in the Baltimore-Washington area (617-259-8776).

The Boston Computer Society (BCS) is a leading microcomputer association, with subgroups for entrepreneurs and consultants. Monthly meetings and electronic bulletin boards provide an excellent way to find and to test out ideas. It is an especially valuable source of the latest entrepreneurial thrusts in microcomputer related hardware and software.

Existing Businesses

The business may not be new, but it is a new venture for the entrepreneur. In addition to the sources noted above, existing business ideas can come from purchasing an ongoing business or acquiring a franchise. In a sense, much of the idea generating process and the work of converting the idea into an opportunity have been accomplished, if the business is operating profitably or has likely future profitability. Such a route to a new venture can be a shortcut, saving time and money, and can reduce the risk as well.

Franchising Ideas. In recent years, between 100 and 300 companies annually have moved into franchising, and the number of franchisors now stands at over 2,000. They account for over 500,000 franchised outlets doing well over $300 billion in sales annually; in fact, the franchise companies account for nearly one-third of all retail sales.

Below is a summary of sources that are a useful start for a search in this field:

Franchise Opportunity Handbook, U.S. Department of Commerce, available from Superintendent of Documents, U.S. Government Printing Office, Washington, D.C. 20402. An annual survey of about 900 franchisors, it contains probably the most extensive information on franchises of any publication. $6.50.

The Franchise Annual Handbook and Directory (Info Press, Edward L. Dixon, ed.) lists about 2,000 American and Canadian franchises in each annual edition. $12.95.

Franchising: Proven Techniques for Rapid Company Expansion and Market Dominance (1980, McGraw-Hill), by David Seltz, discusses how to go about franchising a business to others.

Franchising World is the monthly publication of the International Franchise Association (IFA), the largest association of established franchisors with over 400 member firms (1015 Connecticut Ave., NW, Washington DC 20036). $60 per year.

Franchising Today is a semi-monthly magazine featuring profiles of successful franchisees and franchisors, and developments in franchising (Franchise Technologies, 1201 San Luis Obispo Ave., Hayward CA 94544). $18 per year.

In addition, *INC.* and *Venture* magazines publish an annual listing of franchise opportunities, and run ads monthly for new opportunities in franchising. Similar advertisements can also be found in the *Wall Street Journal.*

Buying an Existing Business. The principal sources of listings of businesses for sale are newspaper and business publications in your area and business brokers. The latter can be found in the yellow pages. Most of their transactions occur in the $25,000 to $200,000 range and include many smaller retail businesses—restaurants and the like. Bank loan officers can be knowledgeable about businesses for sale, as can trust officers. Similarly, bankruptcy judges have a continual flow of ventures in serious trouble. If you have the relevant experience and know-how to operate one of these businesses, there can be some excellent opportunities buried beneath all the financial debris of a bankrupt firm.

One caution, however: the very best private businesses sold are usually not advertised or brokered. Simply put, the real "gems" are usually bought by individuals or firms closest to them: management (if they are not already the owners), directors, customers, suppliers, or financial backers.

In summary, there are a great many useful sources and guidelines for searching for new business ideas, and for locating existing ones. There is a lot of help out there. With the advent of the personal computer, new networks, electronic bulletin boards, and information services will make an increasing part of the search possible from home.

4

Recognizing Opportunity

There are two classes of venture opportunities: those that are profitable and can be harvested, and all the rest. The most successful entrepreneurs and venture capital investors work hard to sort out good opportunities among the myriad of new business ideas that flow their way. They are *opportunity focused.* They know the difference between a good idea and a good opportunity, and can spot it. They start with what customers and the marketplace want, and do not lose sight of it. They concentrate on how to add significant value for that customer.

The good news is that this is a very situational and judgemental process, which means plenty of room for individual initiative. The bad news is that among the 18 million plus businesses in the U.S., only about one venture in 30 is propelled by entrepreneurs good enough at opportunity spotting and executing to grow their ventures to over $1 million in annual sales.

Most entrepreneurs who start a business, particularly if it is their first venture, run out of cash at a faster rate than they bring in customers and profitable sales. There are lots of reasons why this happens, but one thing is for sure: these entrepreneurs have not focused on the right opportunity. Often it is a lack of experience—entrepreneurs who fail initially and learn from the experience usually bounce back and succeed later on.

A sizeable part of the problem is that they lack enough experience in specific market areas and in business. As a result they lack knowledge of the rules of thumb and benchmarks that can guide them in recognizing a good opportunity and saying no to the rest. Take, for instance, an example of one such benchmark from the minicomputer industry: $100,000 or more in sales per employee. Sales of less than $75,000 per employee can mean a company in serious trouble. Interestingly, performance data from sixty computer related start-ups in the U.S. between 1975 and 1984 revealed less than one-third of these firms achieved per-employee sales of $75,000 or more.

There is an enormous flow of ideas and opportunities in our country. Think of a three-dimensional conveyor belt through an open window—your "window on opportunity." The speed at which these opportunities flow is variable—the conveyor belt speeds up, slows down, even changes the rate at which this occurs. The window also is constantly opening and closing, on all four sides, representing the volatile and dynamic nature of the marketplace, changes in technology and competitors' actions.

Given this scenario, the ability to recognize an opportunity when it appears, and the sense of timing to seize it as the window is opening rather than slamming shut, is central to entrepreneurial success. Yet we often hear, especially from young, new entrepreneurs, the exhortation: "Go for it! So what if it doesn't work out. I can do it again. Why wait for a better opportunity?" While there can be no substitute for actually doing it, such itchiness can be a real mistake unless it is focused on a solid opportunity. Why is this so?

Lemons and Plums

It takes considerably longer than most new entrepreneurs might think to determine whether a new venture is a success or a failure. The lemons (losers) ripen in about two-and-a-half years, while the plums (winners) take seven or eight years. (These time frames may be shorter in new, more volatile, and technologically innovative areas.) Realistically, there is a seven to ten year period to which most entrepreneurs must be committed before a capital gain is realizable. An extreme example is a Silicon Valley venture capital group who invested in a new firm in 1966. It was not until early 1984 that the venture was successful enough to sell stock to the public and thereby enable the investors to realize a capital gain.

The implications of this time span are significant for how many ventures one person can take on. Say you are twenty-five years old when you start your first venture. If it is not a good opportunity, or you lack the relevant experience to succeed by yourself—or to attract key people that would make the venture succeed—you will be 27 or 28 by the time you find out it is not working out. You can try again, as many do.

If you fail on the next two you may be going on 35 with very little to show for it. The wear and tear, and burnout, of those failures have probably also ended your first, and maybe your second marriage, if you are like most entrepreneurs who have traveled this rocky road. Attracting the money, people and other support needed to start another company is now very difficult, unless your own pockets are extraordinarily deep. The options become increasingly limited.

Let's say you succeed the second time around. Chances are you will be 35 to 40 by the time you have any realizable personal net worth in the venture. There is plenty of time left to start and grow one or two, maybe even three "plums," or to keep growing the first one, but for most entrepreneurs, no more.

The message is simple enough: successful venture building takes a lot more time than is commonly believed. While there appear to be "boundless opportunities" for those with the entrepreneurial zest, most new entrepreneurs will only be able to seize and attempt to execute a very few. Fortunately, all you need do is grow and harvest one venture whose sales have exceeded several million dollars and is quite profitable. The result will be a satisfying and financially rewarding professional life.

Opportunity First

The best point of departure in selecting a new venture is the opportunity: the customer, marketplace, and industry. *What* is the opportunity you are seeking to seize or create, and *why does it exist*? What are the prevailing market trends, competitors' vulnerabilities, technology, location, regulatory changes, lead times in market and product innovation, and the economics and capital gains potential of the business, that add up to a compelling opportunity? How can you achieve a superior competitive advantage—in technology, timing, management, or barriers to entry (such as know-how or key people)? The opportunity is the most fruitful point of departure. Any other starting point usually places the cart squarely before the horse.

Perhaps the best evidence of cart before the horse comes from the tens of thousands of tax-sheltered investments that turned sour by the mid 1980s. Many entrepreneurs and investors apparently learned the lesson the hard way. A good investment is anchored in fundamental, underlying economic opportunity, not in tax-law loopholes that make the numbers look positive. It is difficult enough to make money in a business trying to earn a profit. To hope to make money in business deals structured to *lose* money is not a sound long-term opportunity.

Obviously it is important that you screen and choose opportunities with great care. Opportunities are situational, and the good ones are anchored in high margin customer needs in an expanding marketplace. For the lead entrepreneur, an attractive opportunity will result in a profitable and harvestable venture that is both *desirable* and *attainable* by the entrepreneur and the management team. In short, if you do not really want it, and cannot really execute it—now—then it's not a good opportunity for you.

How do You Spot a Good Opportunity?

The real potential of many start-up opportunities is frequently *inversely* related to the data available about market characteristics, shares, competitors, and so on. When these facts and numbers are available, or can be purchased, you can be sure lots of entrepreneurs and competitors will also obtain them. This is one reason why the entrepreneur's vision and experience is so important in sensing an opportunity. It is that creative eye to see how a pattern of success in one field can lead to a successful new firm in another business, such as adapting neoprene body suits for skin diving to surfing, and then to neoprene for fisherman's waders or swim suits. Not only will the data be full of gaps, inaccuracies and contradictions, it will be ambiguous in its meaning. The entrepreneur can see linkages and possibilities, where the perfectionist and the timid see chaos and contradiction, and the latter fail to grasp the opportunity and act on it.

What is behind the batting averages of successful entrepreneurs? What factors do they pay particular attention to in order to spot and seize an opportunity, at the right time? How do they create what may be perceived by others as an unfair advantage?

One useful way to answer these questions is to examine some of the benchmarks used by highly successful entrepreneurs and their venture capital backers to evaluate start-up businesses—although these principles and benchmarks are not the exclusive domain of venture capitalists. They are simply "good business," and are well known to experienced and successful entrepreneurs in a wide range of businesses that do not have venture capital backing. By knowing them, it is possible to be more selective in screening opportunities, and thereby improve the odds of success.

Benchmarks for Investing

Usually, the first contact between an entrepreneur and investor is when the entrepreneur calls or forwards a business plan. The investor's initial screening of the opportunity zeroes in on the benchmarks noted here. These same criteria need to be tempered and adjusted to meet your personal goals and situation. The issues are simple enough: Is there a strong, experienced lead entrepreneur and team? Is there a significant opportunity? Is there a significant capital gains potential?

• Do the lead entrepreneur and team possess the capacities, relevant experience, commitment, vision and entrepreneurial zest to execute the opportunity? These judgements evolve by meeting and working with the founders, and usually are not based solely on a fifteen or twenty-minute phone call. Clearly, if you do not want partners then you may have to settle for a business that can be run and digested solo.

• Are customers and market segment(s) or niche(s) clearly identified? Have prototypes of the product or service gained the enthusiasm of some customers to the point that they readily share their enthusiasm with other prospective customers and investors? Ideally, they have provided "free" space, people and other resources to enable the product or service to be brought to market sooner. They may agree to advance payments, provide R&D contracts, and possibly even invest in the venture. All those actions clearly signal that the venture is meeting an important customer need, with high value-added benefits to the customer and end user, and the customers are receptive to innovation.

• Is the market size $50–100 million or or more? This means that significant sales can be achieved early on with a non-threatening market share, roughly 5% or less. A $1 million sales level would require a 1% market share or less.

The market can be too large as well, implying a maturity, stability and a level of certainty that translates into lower margins and profitability, and competition from large firms. Consider the entry of Apple Computer into the microcomputer industry in 1975, compared to a new entrant in 1985.

Conversely, domination of a smaller market can still build a very profitable venture with significant harvest potential, even though it is not attractive as a venture capital investment.

• Is the market growing at an annual rate of 30% to 50% or more? This creates a lot of niches for new entrants. It means the industry, though a bit chaotic, is thriving, up-beat, looking ahead to opportunities—rather than concentrating on the defensive moves against competitors that often characterize mature, slowly growing industries. If a $100 million market is growing at 50% yearly, a new venture can attain first year sales of $1 million by capturing just 2% of the increase.

Such growth also means the market will be a billion dollar plus industry in a few years and have plenty of room for innovative entrants who can achieve sales of $50-100 million, or more. If you understand the opportunity, and have the commitment and relevant experience to execute it, $1 million is a realistic sales level. COMPAQ, the portable microcomputer firm, achieved sales of $110 million in its very first year!

• Are the gross margins 40 to 50% or more? There is nothing more forgiving to an entrepreneur than high and durable gross margins (the unit selling price less all direct, variable costs). Once the gross margin exceeds 50% there is a tremendous cushion built in that permits more errors, mistakes, and steep learning curves than is possible with gross margins of 20% or less. Think of it this way: If gross margins are 20%, for every $1 increase in fixed costs (insurance, salaries, rent, utilities, etc.) there must be a sales increase of $5 to stay at the same profit level. If gross margins are 50%, however, a $1 dollar increase in fixed costs requires a sales increase of just $2, instead of $5.

• The first important corollary to high gross margins is that they are also rewarding. Such high margins often translate into strong and durable profit after taxes of at least 10%, and often 15% to 20% or more. Compare these figures with the the 500 largest service companies, who earned net income as a percent of sales typically in the 3-5% range—and outperformed the top 500 industrial group.

• This leads to the second corollary—higher earnings per share and higher return on stockholder's equity. The higher the after-tax earnings the greater the potential harvest price of a company, and thus the capital gain, whether it is sold through an initial public offering (IPO), is acquired, or is sold privately. (Note: comparative financial performance ratios for businesses in the field you are considering can be found in the Robert Morris Associates annual statements.)

• Can the business achieve a positive cash flow rapidly, or within one to two years?

• Can you gain personal control over the necessary start-up capital and resources, even though you may not own them outright?

• Is there a dominant competitor in the marketplace, such as Coca-Cola and PepsiCola in soft drinks? A market share of 40%, 50%, and especially 60% or more usually implies power and influence over suppliers, customers, pricing, and cost curves that create serious barriers and risks for a new firm.

If the dominant competitor is at full capacity, and is lethargic to innovate or to add capacity in a large and growing market, then there may be an entry opportunity. Unfortunately, entrepreneurs usually do not find such sleepy competition in dynamic, emerging industries dense with opportunity. If the market leader has a 20% share or less, a new entrant is not so vulnerable to brute force and bullying. It is also less likely that the leader has the power to erect barriers to your entry and growth.

• Will the new firm have an "unfair" advantage? A significant response and lead time, or window, in terms of technological superiority, proprietary protection, location, key people, plant capacity, market innovation, or distribution, is important, especially in high-technology ventures. Such an unfair advantage is often achieved by a proprietary product or service, or one that is very difficult to imitate, and cannot be reverse-engineered, or by having the very best people. These advantages can create barriers to entry or expansion by others. Determining lead time necessitates a good approximation of how fast you and your competitors can respond.

Fatal Flaws

A lot of opportunities appear promising at first glance. Many of the above criteria are met, but there is a "fatal flaw" in the venture. Consider the following examples of fatal flaws:

Very small market for the product. One inventor devised an electronic switch which would enable the user to interconnect a personal computer, the home burglar alarm, and the thermostat. At the time there simply were not enough customers who would buy such a device. It can be all too easy to be either too early or too late in recognizing an opportunity window.

Overpowering competition and a high cost of entry. The U.S. automobile industry has examples of ill-fated attempts to enter the industry: Tucker in the late 1940s, Bricklin in the 1970s, and Delorean in the 1980s. In the 1980s airline deregulation has invited many new entrants, and we can expect casualties there as well.

Lack of distribution. Air Florida was unable to get its flights listed in the computers of travel agents nationwide, and could not generate the sales to survive.

Not producing at a competitive price. An example of this was Bowmar's inability to remain competitive in electronic calculators after the producers of large-scale integrated circuits, such as Hewlett-Packard, entered the business. Being unable to achieve and sustain a position as a low-cost producer shortens the life expectancy of the new venture.

Lack of influence and control over product development and component prices. The entrepreneur has very little control over these if a crucial state-of-the-art component is manufactured and supplied elsewhere. Vertical integration is the usual way to gain control of parts and supplies and secure margins.

Inability to expand beyond one product. This is often a firm driven by an inventor or technical innovator rather than by an entrepreneur. Perhaps the leading example of this flaw is the failure of Osborne portable computers. After reaching over 1000 employees it collapsed in the face of new competition. At this writing, its successor, COMPAQ, may be vulnerable to the same shortcoming.

Overwhelming financial requirements. Recently, a team of undergraduate college students proposed to develop a business plan to enter the satellite repair business. Aside from the experience question, their research indicated that the required start-up capital was in the $50 to $200 million range. Projects of this magnitude are the domain of government and the mega-corporation, rather than independent entrepreneurs and venture capitalists.

The opportunity cannot be harvested profitably. Most opportunities become jobs for the self-employed, rather than companies with the value and durability to attract buyers. If the venture lacks a sufficient level of the criteria noted previously, the chances of realizing a capital gain diminish rapidly. In that event, you may have a "job," but you cannot really get out of the venture in any responsible or financially rewarding way, so you had better love it. In short, it is much easier to get into a business than to get out successfully. How many small-scale entrepreneurs have you heard that consider themselves stuck in just such a situation? The owner of a quite successful sporting goods store in a wealthy town was overheard recently confiding in a friend: "It's really an excellent living, but it is so boring doing the same thing each day; it gets to you."

Risks, Rewards and Trade-offs

One of the most challenging parts of the opportunity "juggling act" is figuring out what the balance is likely to be among risks, rewards and trade-offs to decide if, in fact, the opportunity is a fit. In doing so, the following are worth considering.

• If the financial exposure in launching a venture is greater than the entrepreneur's net worth, the resources available, and the alternative disposable earnings stream if it does not work out, the deal may be too big for now. Unless it is virtually certain to succeed, the founder is unwittingly buying a ticket to future bankruptcy. And while today's bankruptcy laws are extremely generous, what about the psychological burdens of living through such an ordeal? Most who have, agree that the emotional cost is infinitely more painful than the financial consequences.

• What is the opportunity cost of pursuing a new venture? If the entrepreneur is good enough to grow a successful, multi-million dollar venture, his talents will be highly valued by established firms as well. More than ever before, larger firms are aggressively and creatively seeking entrepreneurs who can manage. Taking a serious look at those potential "golden handcuff" alternatives is an important part of sizing up any opportunity.

Take, for instance, a young entrepreneur we shall call George Hill. Between the ages of 23 and 29 he played a lead role in starting and growing two firms. Each attained sales over $5 million in five years. Neither was particularly profitable, and the second, which George launched on his own, closed in the third year. When he began a search for a new job, he found a very enthusiastic reception. Although his second venture was not successful, and the first one cannot be harvested, his entrepreneurial experiences were most unusual. As one observer put it: "He is 29 with the experience of a 50 year old." The most he had ever earned a year in his own venture was about $60,000. He had several job offers in the six figure plus range.

• The opportunities an entrepreneur elects to pursue will shape him as a businessman and person in ways it is hard to imagine. Further, these experiences will position him, for better or for worse, for the next opportunity. In the early years, it is important to gain the relevant management and profit and loss experience.

Last, the trade-offs are personal. A good opportunity is one that fits with how and where the entrepreneur wants to work and live. The title of the play tells us, "You Can't Take it With You." On the other hand, the wealthy French Baron de Rothchild observed: "You can either eat well, or you can sleep well!" By implication, you cannot do both.

5

Sources for Opportunity Screening

Fortunately, there seems to be no shortage of sources to aid in screening opportunities and analyzing markets. A huge array of information, directories, databases, and other sources of market and competitor intelligence are now available, affordable and accessible from homes and offices. What follows is a summary of leading sources, data services, and conventional ways of gathering competitor intelligence. In the next chapter is a run-down of on-line information services.

Trade Associations and Periodicals

Almost every industry has a trade association and a periodical. They are some of the best sources of data about a specific industry. Trade journals print, on a regular basis, market surveys and forecasts. Moreover, the advertisements in trade journals provide an excellent source of information about competitors and their products. Attendance at trade association meetings and conversations with sales representatives are also good ways of assessing the competition.

The trade associations and journals of various industries can be found in:

Encyclopedia of Associations
(Vol. 1, National Organizations of the United States)
Gale Research Company
Book Tower
Detroit, Michigan 48226

Ayer Directory of Newspapers, Magazines and Trade Publications:
Ayer Press
West Washington Square
Philadelphia, Pennsylvania 19106

General Marketing Data Sources

In addition to the trade journals, data on the market size and trends in a great many industries can be found in:

Predicasts Basebook

Predicast, Inc.
200 University Circle Research Center
11001 Cedar Avenue
Cleveland, Ohio 11106

U.S. Industrial Outlook

U.S. Department of Commerce
Superintendent of Documents
Government Printing Office
Washington, D.C. 20402

Predicasts Basebook publishes abstracts of forecasts for U.S. statistics as well as those for a large number of industries and detailed products.

Sources of Market Studies

In addition to these broad-coverage data sources, market studies of particular industries and products are available from:

Predicasts
200 University Circle Research Center
11001 Cedar Avenue
Cleveland, Ohio 11106

Arthur D. Little
25 Acorn Park
Cambridge, Massachusetts 02140

Business Communications Company
471 Glenbrook Road
Stamford, Connecticut 06906

Frost & Sullivan, Inc.
106 Fulton Street
New York, New York 10038

Morton Research Corp.
1745 Merrick Ave.
Merrick, New York 11566

Theta Technology Corp.
Peer Building
530 Silas Beane Hwy.
Wethersfield, Connecticut 06109

Prices of the studies and reports provided by these organizations range from $50 to $600. Further, for $150 Predicast will custom-search their library of a half-million abstracts and provide 300 abstracts that are most relevant to a market research need.

Consumer Expenditures

Data on consumer expenditures at many places in the country can be found in:

Editor & Publisher Market Guide
Editor & Publisher Company
850 Third Avenue
New York, New York 10022

U.S. Census Reports
Census of Business
Census of Housing
Census of Population
U.S. Bureau of Census
Superintendent of Documents
U.S. Government Printing Office
Washington, D.C. 20402

Survey of Buying Power
Sales Management, Inc.
630 Third Avenue
New York, New York 10017

Financial Ratios

Information on the financial ratios for various industries that can be useful in evaluating competitive operating practices can be found in:

Annual Statement Studies
Robert Morris Associates

Philadelphia Bank Building
Philadelphia, Pennsylvania 19107

Almanac of Business & Industrial Financial Ratios
Leo Troy
Prentice-Hall
Englewood Cliffs, New Jersey

Guide to Market Data

For an overall guide to sources of data on consumer and industrial markets, see:

Data Sources for Business & Market Analysis
Nathalie D. Frank
Scarecrow Press, Inc.
52 Liberty Street, P.O. Box 656
Metuchen, New Jersey 08840

If you wish to conduct a limited sampling of your potential market, you might find useful the note, "Direct Marketing Information for Entrepreneurs," developed at Babson College by Professor Robert Ronstadt and Nancy Tieken, and available from Lord Publishing, Dover, Massachusetts 02030.

Guides to Journal Articles

Journals and periodicals are a large and excellent source of data on products, industries, and markets. The title of an article can be a good clue to what it's about. Some useful directories to articles—available in most libraries—are:

Readers Guide to Periodical Literature
Business Periodicals Index
Applied Science and Technology Index

Directories

The most comprehensive listing of directories is the *Directory of Directories,* which contains a thoroughly described and completely indexed compilation of over 5,000 directories. It contains all types of rosters, directories, industrial guides and lists.

Directory of Directories

Gale Research Company
Book Tower
Detroit, Michigan 48226
313-961-2242

Also available from the same source is the *Encyclopedia of Business Information Sources*. It contains specific listings of specilized encyclopedias, handbooks, abstract services, trade association, manuals, and listing of on-line data bases.

Data Services

Association of Computer Users
P. O. Box 9003
Boulder, Colorado 80301
(303) 499-1722

Like a "Consumer Reports of Computers," the Association of Computer Users makes available reports on the quality of computers in the $15,000 to $50,000 price range. Reports examine individual machines and are written especially for business users. A dozen reports can vary in price from $150 to $450. Membership is $25.

Bottomline Management Association
10 E 40th Street
New York, New York 10016
(212) 683-5353

Bottomline Management Association sponsors a "dial-an-answer" service on payroll-related problems. Questions concerning payroll taxes, insurance, equal employment opportunity, employee benefits, and recxruitment are answered as often as the need arises. The cost of the service is $150 per year. The fee includes regular bulletins which analyze common business problems.

Business Growth Services
General Electric Company
120 Erie Blvd., Dept. 392

Schenectady, New York 12305
(518) 385-2577

Business Growth Services provides information on new businesses or products immediately available for acquisition or licensing. Its "New Product/New Business Digest" discloses over 500 unique new products and processes developed by both small and large companies; these new business ventures did not fit General Electric's product lines. The digest costs $45.

Bureau of the Census, Current Industrial Reports
Subscriber Services Section, Publications
Bureau of the Census
Washington D.C. 20233
(301) 763-7472

Current Industrial Reports provides shipment and sales data for over 100 industries. Tables include data on imports, exports, and shipments, with breakdowns within industries.

Findex
Find/SVP
500 Fifth Avenue
New York, New York 10036
(212) 354-2424

Findex is a directory of market research reports, studies, and surveys updated every six months. Findex contains descriptions of over 4,000 reports available from 200 publishers, including the publication date, price, and instructions for obtaining copies. These reports cover a wide range of industries and businesses, with published research on such things as developing technology trends as well as changes in foreign markets. Findex costs $115 annually.

The Information Bank
Advertising and Marketing Intelligence
Mount Pleasant Office Park
1719-A Route 10

Parsippany, New Jersey 07054
(201) 539-5850

The Information Bank, which is part of the New York Times Company, consists of a data base of sixty major worldwide publications, including business and financial journals. Advertising and Marketing Intelligence (AMI) consists of trade journals and public relations statements relating to the advertising and marketing areas. Information for both data bases is current within a few days. Any topic or combination of topics can be researched to yield abstracts of relevant newspaper and magazine articles.

Applications of this service vary from marketing trend analysis to international finance. For example, topics such as trends in do-it-yourself home improvement and import-export activity could be quite important to certain small businesses. Other uses might be gathering information on prospective merger, acquisition, or takeover candidates.

Both data bases are available to small business on a fee-for-service basis. The Parsippany office can offer advice on what is available. Research can be performed and an abstract sent the same day. Full text copies of articles are also available.

The fee for basic research is $110 per hour. A typical run is usually 12 minutes, or $22.

Information Data Search, Inc.
1463 Beacon Street
Brookline, Massachusetts 02146
(617) 232-1393

Information Data Search (IDS) bills itself as "a modern, one-stop research and information center equipped to answer virtually any question you have on a wide variety of subjects, technical or general." IDS has access to more than 100 computer data bases nationwide and thus is in a position to choose those most likely to yield information customers request. Costs of the service vary according to the project, with quotes offered before research begins. IDS says a typical range for services is $14 to $500.

Lockheed DIALOG Information Retrieval Service
3460 Hillview Avenue
Palo Alto, California 94304
(800) 227-1927, in California (800) 982-5838

The DIALOG service offers access to more than 30 million journal and newspaper articles, conference papers, and reports from over 100 data bases covering all areas of science, technology, business, medicine, social science, current affairs, and humanities. One example of its application might be for marketing a device for the handicapped. An entrepreneur could search a medical data base to ascertain product need and search a business data base to determine the present state of the market, including competition, dollar sales, and market share.

Department of Commerce Publications

Superintendent of Documents
U.S. Government Printing Office
Washington D.C. 20402
(202) 783-3238

The U.S. Department of Commerce publishes reports that can help small-business owners plan their marketing efforts. The reports are inexpensive and are often found at local libraries. Major Department of Commerce reports include:

The U.S. Industrial Outlook. Contains reports on 200 industries. Important industry developments and patterns are discussed along with statistics on such things as the total value of shipments, number of establishments with more than 200 employees and less than 20 employees, exports, and annual rates of change. The 1980 *U.S. Industrial Outlook* contained a section on opportunities for small business in the 1980s.

County Business Patterns. Contains statistics on the number of businesses, by type, in each county. Specific employment and payroll data is included. The number of establishments, broken into nine categories based on number of employees, is also given for each industry.

NASA Industrial Application Centers

Several universities have information centers to provide technically oriented reports, studies, and literature searches. They provide access to over 150 data banks and National Aeronautics and Space Administration (NASA) research. A typical bibliography with 250 to 300 sources costs $100, but fees may range from $30 to thousands of dollars. Fees are discussed before research begins. The information centers are as follows:

Technology Use Studies Center
Southeastern Oklahoma State University
Durant, Oklahoma 74701

Technology Applications Center
University of New Mexico
Albuquerque, New Mexico 87131

Western Research Application Center
University of Southern California
University Park, Los Angeles, California 90007

New England Research Applications Center
Mansfield Professional Park
Storrs, Connecticut 06268

North Carolina Science and Technology Research Center
P.O. Box 12235
Research Triangle Park, North Carolina 27709

Knowledge Availability Systems Center
University of Pittsburgh
Pittsburgh, Pennsylvania 15260

Aerospace Research Application Center
Administration Building
1201 E. 38th Street
Indianapolis, Indiana 47401

Conventional Competitor Intelligence

Would you like to know your what your competitors' sales plans are, the key elements of their corporate strategies, the capacity and technology of their plants, who their principal suppliers and customers are, and the new products they have under development—without breaking any laws to know? Not only would you like it, you *must* have such intelligence in order to assess an opportunity, its risks and trade-offs.

Getting competitive information in an emerging industry is probably more difficult than in a mature field. Nonetheless, a wide range of conventional practices can help you find out what you need to know about what is happening in the industry, the market and with customers.

Trade shows and conferences are a prime place to pick brains and to discover the latest activities of competitors. It is always amazing how much proprietary information is leaked in casual conversation by engineers, scientists, and salesmen who cannot resist bragging about their latest breakthroughs or initiatives.

Hiring people away from competitors is a frequent occurrence today. To legally challenge the hiring, competitors must prove that your company hired the person intentionally to get specific trade secrets. A flurry of information-gathering by that person immediately prior to resignation is circumstantial evidence of this intention.

Consulting firms interviewing competitors claim to be conducting an industry study, and promise to share the data they develop. Some of the biggest consulting firms get information for their clients this way.

Debriefing design consultants can pay off in fields like computers or software, where competitors frequently use the same consultants.

Debriefing competitors' former employees can often provide information damaging to a competitor, especially if the employee departed on bad terms.

Encouraging key customers, suppliers and buyers to talk, a lot, is another tactic used to learn as much as possible about the competition.

Obtaining Freedom of Information Act filings can reveal a surprising amount of information from competitors who are doing business with the government. This can be done discreetly through a company which processes such inquiries: FOI Services, Inc., Rockville, Maryland.

Doing reverse engineering can determine costs of production and sometimes even manufacturing methods. One company learned first hand about such tactics. No sooner had it announced a patented new product than it received 50 orders, half of which were from competitors asking for only one or two of the items. (Filing a patent can negate a significant market lead-time over competitors).

6

On-Line Databases

The explosive growth in microcomputers and networks in the past few years has led to enormous growth in the availability of on-line databases and information sources. A word of caution: the "garbage in-garbage out" rule certainly applies to using any database. Unless you know what you are looking for and your questions focused, you may spend more time and money than you can afford. You may dig out loads of useful and interesting information that is not *essential* to assessing your opportunity and shaping a marketing strategy.

Directory of On-Line Databases
Caudra Associates, Inc.
2001 Wilshire Blvd., Suite 305
Santa Monica, California 90403

The *Directory of On-Line Databases* lists about 270 on-line services carrying nearly 1,800 databases produced by 900 organizations. Suppliers of these information services usually charge $50 to $100 per hour of usage, and some charge a modest sign-up fee of about $50.

Probably the most complete and comprehensive book of listings available is

The Computer Data and Database Source Book, by Mathew Lesko
Avon Books
1790 Broadway
New York, New York 10019

Two of the most significant sources of business information are DIALOG, provided by Lockheed, and Data Resources, Inc. (DRI) databases, containing over 10 million time series as far back as 1929. The list below summarizes other on-line data bases (from *Personal Software,* June 1984, p. 126).

The second list (*Personal Software*, p. 127) names the principal links to these various sources of data, such as The Source, Compuserve, Dow-Jones News/Retrieval, and Dialog Information Services.

Some On-Line Databases

Accountants Index (Accounting)
American Institute of Certified Public Accountants
On-line through SDC Search Service
Adtrack (Advertising)
Corporate Intelligence, Inc.
On-line through Dialog International
Agricola (Literature on agriculture)
U.S. Department of Agriculture
On-line through BRS, Dialog Information Services, Inc.
Agriculture Bank (Agricultural economic data)
Data Resources, Inc.
On-line through Data Resources, Inc.
American Profiles (Demographics and population in U.S.)
Donnelley Marketing
On-line through Dun & Bradstreet Control Data Corp/ Business Information Systems
Balance of Payments (International finance)
International Monetary Fund
On-line through Chase Econometrics/Interactive Data
Billboard Information Network (Music and music industry)
Billboard Publications, Inc.
On-line through Billboard Publications, Inc.
Book Review Index (Social science and humanities)
Gale Research Company
On-line through BRS, Dialog Information Services, Inc.
Books In Print (Books and periodicals)
R. R. Bowker Company
On-line through BRS, Dialog Information Services, Inc.
CSS/QUOTES+ (Securities, Canada and U.S.)
Dun & Bradstreet

On-line through Dun & Bradstreet Computer Services
Commodities Futures (Commodities, U.S.)
Call Computer, Inc.
On-line through Call Computer, Inc.
Compuserve Consumer Information Services (Multifaceted information services providing many data bases)
CompuServe, Inc.
On-line through CompuServe, Inc.
Compuserve Executive Information Services (Multifaceted information services providing many data bases)
CompuServe, Inc.
On-line through CompuServe, Inc.
Dow Jones News and Dow Jones Free-Text (Business and industry news, economics and finance)
Dow Jones & Co.
On-line through Dow Jones & Co.
EEI Capsule (Economics, U.S.)
Evans Economics, Inc.
On-line through Control Data Corp./ Business Information Services/Boeing Computer Services Co.
Foundations (Directory of funding sources and awards)
The Foundation Center
On-line through Dialog Information Services, Inc.
Harvard Business Review (Business Management)
HBR/Online
On-line through John Wiley & Sons, Inc.
HORSE (Horse breeding)
Bloodstock Research Information Services, Inc.
On-line through Bloodstock Research Information Services, Inc.
International Software Data Base (Computers and computer industry)
Imprint Software Ltd.
On-line through Dialog Information Services, Inc.

Legal Resource Index (Law)
Information Access Corp.
On-line through Dialog Information Services, Inc.
Legi-Slate (U.S. Government, Federal and State)
Legi-Slate, Inc.
On-line through Legi-Slate Inc.
Medline (Biomedicine)
Australian Medicine Network, BLAISE-LINK, DRS
On-line through Dialog Information Services, Inc., DATA-STAR, DIVDI, MC-KBIC, National Library of Medicine, Japan Information Center of Science & Information Technology
Microcomputer Index (Computers)
Microcomputer Information Services
On-line through Dialog Information Services, Inc.
National Technical Information Service (Science and Technology)
National Technical Information Services
On-Line through BRS, CISTI; DATA-STAR; Dialog Information Services; ESA-IRS; INKA Karlsruche; SDC Information Services CEDOCAR
Sociological Abstracts (Sociology)
Sociological Abstracts, Inc.
On-line through BRS; DATA-STAR; Dialog Information Services, Inc.
The Source (many information services)
Source Telecomputing Corp.
On-line through The Source
Standard and Poor's Industry Financial Data Bank (U.S. business and industry finance)
Data Resources, Inc., Standard and Poor's Corp.
On-line through Data Resources Corp.

7

Opportunity Screening Guide

Greater than the tread of mighty armies is an idea whose time has come.

—Victor Hugo

The opportunity screening guide is a specific method of opportunity recognition and evaluation. With it, you can apply benchmarks, criteria and screening methods used by successful entrepreneurs and venture capitalists to evaluate your own venture idea and lay the foundations for preparing a business plan.

What is the Opportunity Screening Guide?

Getting the odds of success in your favor necessitates finding the right opportunity, in the right place, at the right time—no small challenge. In order to describe the business accurately, and to develop a sound entry and growth strategy, you need a clear vision and conception of the opportunity. Further, your understanding of the market, production, distribution, service and financial aspects of the venture should be sufficiently concrete to determine if it is attractive enough to pursue.

Involving potential partners or team members in the screening task is an excellent way to try out the "marriage"—to find out if you can work together well. It will also speed up the process, which is likely to take a minimum of 20 to 30 hours of effort, even with a team. Of course, if a team is not for you, you can savor this task solo.

Opportunity Conditions

Once you have completed the following sections of the guide, you can prepare this summary, usually one to two pages, with key points which address the questions below.

What are the compelling conditions and circumstances propelling the opportunity? Why does the opportunity exist, now, for you? A sound concept will be technically feasible, add significant value to the customer or end user, enjoy some significant competitive advantages, and have a large and durable potential pay-off compared to the time and cost required to develop and execute it.

What is the evidence and reasoning that leads you to conclude you can seize or create the opportunity?

Do you have any special or "unfair" competitive advantages over competitors or substitutes?

What is the opportunity window and its perishability?

What is it about the economics, the market conditions, trends, competitors' vulnerabilities and your capabilities and advantages that make the opportunity attractive, and why?

What are the prospects that the venture can be harvested—if that is your ultimate goal—and are the risks, rewards and trade-offs acceptable to the founders? If it cannot be harvested, is the profitability both durable and sufficient enough to meet your goals?

Is the management team convinced that the outcome of executing the opportunity is desirable, and that they are able to attain it?

What entry strategy suits the opportunity?

Can you achieve control or use of the minimum resources necessary to pursue the opportunity?

Usually these points are not clear at first—most concepts are ill-defined to begin with, which is normal and acceptable. If you have worked through the other issues, and the answers to these questions still elude you, are fuzzy, or cannot be articulated, it is time to look for a better opportunity.

Description of the Product, Service or Activity

What is the business you want to enter? Describe the concept clearly in twenty-five words or less.

What products, services or activities will be sold, and what are their eventual end uses? (If available, attach photos and specifications or descriptions.)

How perishable is it, and what are the likely windows on obsolescence?

What is the development status of the product or service? Do you have a prototype, sample of work, or demonstration disk (if software)?

How much time and money do you estimate it will take to develop, test it with customers, and introduce it to the market, license it, or open for business? Or, if the business is further along, what results and potential orders have emerged from initial customer tests or trials?

For intellectual property or proprietary products, what is the status of any copyrights, trade secrets, or patents, and what needs to be done (actions, time, money) to assure its protection?

Who are the primary customer groups, and what are the main reasons why they will buy your product or service?

What on-going service, maintenance and customer support is needed, such as warranty, repair, training, or other?

Describe objectively the strengths and weaknesses of the product, service or business activity. Whether or not you plan to seek outside financing to execute the opportunity, it is vital to have a realistic view of the vulnerabilities and fragilities of your venture, as well as its strengths.

At this point, it is possible that you ought to abandon or alter your venture's product or service idea. A realistic estimate of the amount of money and time needed to get the product or service to market, or be open for business, may be beyond your own limits. Even in the abundant venture capital market of the mid and late 1980s, only 1% to 3% of all proposals received funding. Typically, the first round of financing is in the $1–2 million range, and to raise over $5 million you need a truly exceptional management team, and a concept whose potential rewards are large or durable compared to the risks and vulnerabilities. The life expectancies of today's technology-based products can be as brief as three years.

Market and Customer Issues

To be an attractive investment, a company should be selling to a market that is large and growing—where a small market share can produce a significant sales volume. The company's competition should be profitable but not so strong as to be overwhelming. And the venture's product must have features and a sales price that will enable it to penetrate the market, and/or solve significant customer problems with competitive products; e.g., poor quality, late delivery, poor service.

Alternatively, a company that can achieve a dominant position over competitors in a smaller and slower growing market is also attractive to some investors.

The purpose of a preliminary market evaluation is to obtain hard facts about the market potential for the venture's product or service, assess the competition, and evaluate what is required to bring and sell the product or service to the customer. Such an analysis is not meant to be precise or comprehensive, but it should serve to eliminate those venture ideas with obvious market difficulties. If the potential payback or value added for customer cannot be identified, or is longer than a year or so, then the idea lacks high profit potential.

Total Market Size and Trends. What is the approximate size of the total potential market for your kind of product or service? Show past, present, and future market size in units and dollars. (Use available market data to estimate a range of values.) If you intend to sell only in a local area, region, or state, identify the area and show only its market data.

Indicate the sources of data, comment on the accuracy of the data, and say who did the market research.

Customer and Market Research. Who are your prospective customers? Can you identify and list them, including names, addresses, and phone numbers? Can you characterize the primary groups, segments or niches you are seeking? Have you, or a team member, sold directly (face to face, by telephone or mail) to these customers?

Assume you have picked 100 persons at random out of a crowd—at a trade show, for instance. What are the 5 to 10 most crucial questions you would like them to answer, and the facts and information you need to know about them in order to identify them as good customer prospects?

Why would they buy from you? What are the compelling advantages, benefits and added value of your product, service or activity? How long before the customer realizes the value? (Less than a year, and you have a winner; over three years won't do.)

How do they buy competitive or substitute products now, e.g., from a direct sales force, wholesale, retail, through manufacturer's reps or brokers, catalog, direct mail, etc.?

Conduct a customer survey, preferably face-to-face, or by phone. This is one of the first interactions to test your idea with potential customers. Summarize your surveys as answers to these questions:
What are the needs you can meet or problems you can solve?
What is the nature of their business or role?
What is the reaction to your idea (positive and negative)?
What questions have they raised?
What specific needs and uses are they seeking?
What are an acceptable selling price, service and support, other key terms?
What is the time frame for their purchase decision?
What are names of competitive firms and products/services?

Describe the buying decision process: who does it, what and who are the influences on the buyer, where does it occur, and how long does it take from first contact to a close, delivery and cash receipt?

Preliminary Market Plan. Make a realistic estimate of sales and market share for the first five years. Note: If your business will be done in one city, state, or region, be sure that your market data applies to the area in which you intend to sell and service. Refer to the sources described earlier, especially Predicasts and County Business Patterns.

What pricing strategies are workable, and how do you plan to position your pricing, given your level of quality, service and probable marketing expenditures? Remember, low prices usually mean lower margins, and less forgiving and rewarding economics.

How do you plan to sell your products (direct, by mail order, phone, reps, etc.)? What are the likely sales, marketing and advertising/ trade promotion costs? How will this be done?

How do you plan to ship and distribute your products? Are there any special requirements (e.g., refrigeration, speed)? How significant are shipping and distribution costs as a percentage of sales and total costs (e.g., is your product transportation-sensitive)?

The single largest factor contributing to stillborn ventures, and failure, is lack of opportunity and lack of market focus. If you were unable to respond to many of these questions, or do not have much of an idea how to answer them, then you have a problem. For one thing, you may have a bad case of "marketing myopia"—especially common among engineers and technologists. For another, you may lack the experience to tackle the venture at this stage. Or you are simply not as far along as you had thought, and have a lot of work ahead if you want the odds in your favor.

Competitive Advantage Issues

Are there other kinds of products or services that compete for the same business with the same customers? (e.g., a hospital uses both mercury and electronic thermometers.) If this is the case, what are the competing products or services?

List your major competitors in order of their reputed share of the market. Comment on who is the pricing leader, quality leader, most innovative, growing most rapidly, most aggressive, having problems.

For each competitor listed, describe in as much detail as you can their marketing tactics in terms of sales force, normal terms of sale, advertising and promotion tactics, distribution and service. How good is their management? How good are their key people?

For the product/service you plan to sell, what prices do competitors charge—at retail level, wholesale level, distributor level, other channel, manufacturing level?

How profitable are these competitors?

Can you be price-competitive and make a good profit? Why?

Do you have to charge prices similar to those of your would-be competitors? Why or why not?

Estimate your unit profit:

Selling Price	$__________	%_____
Variable Costs*	$__________	%_____
Gross Margin	$__________	%_____
Fixed Operating Costs	$__________	%_____
Profit Before Taxes	$__________	%_____

* These are fixed for each unit and consist of direct labor, materials, shipping and distribution, or the purchase cost of a product or component that is resold.

What are the industry averages for these budget line items? Use Robert Morris Associates, Dun & Bradstreet, or actual data you may have to see how your estimates compare.

How much can you control and influence prices and costs among customers, suppliers and the channels of distribution? How do you plan to achieve this leverage?

Which competitors enjoy cost advantages and economies of scale in production, advertising and marketing, and distribution? What are the prospects and time-cost constraints to become the low-cost producer and distributor?

Do you enjoy, or can you gain, advantages in response and lead times in terms of technology, capacity changes, product and market innovation?

Do you enjoy, or can you gain any legal or contractual edges such as proprietary protection, or other market exclusivity such as specific franchise or distributor rights?

How are competitors fragile and vulnerable, and what is the time window that can be exploited? They may be in disarray from loss of key people, have suffered a recent legal suit involving extensive top-management time, or have simply failed to innovate, and need too much time to catch up.

Do you enjoy, or can you gain "unfair advantages" in strategic, technological, regulatory, people, resource, location or other factors?

What are the financial strengths and weaknesses of competitor and industry benchmarks? Use industry data for your business, and include any specific data you can about your competitors.

Economics and Harvest Issues

What gross margins do you anticipate (selling price less direct, variable costs)? Margins of 40% to 50% or more are attractive, and under 20% unattractive. Less than very generous margins leave no room or time for learning from mistakes.

How attractive and durable are the cash flow and profit streams? What is the basis for your conclusions?

What is your estimate of profitability after taxes, months to breakeven, positive cash flow and return on equity?

What is your best estimate of the capital required to seize the opportunity and to attain breakeven sales? To attain your five-year sales estimates?

Prepare a preliminary quarterly cash-flow statement for the first two years (save time and effort by using a microcomputer spreadsheet program). This will enable you to estimate how much money is required to launch the business.

Start-up Capital Requirements

For the following start-up items, estimate the range of funds needed and the date each expenditure will occur:

- Plant, equipment and facilities.
- Product development, prototype or demonstration package, user documentation or manuals.
- Market research.
- Setup of sales and distribution.
- One-time fees or expenditures (e.g., initial inventory, legal costs for preparing contracts or agreements).
- Lease deposits or other pre-payments.
- Salaries, rent, phone, insurance premiums for key persons, and other overhead that must be committed before the firm achieves a positive cash flow.
- Sales and demo trips to trade shows, customers, media for product introduction.
- Up-front marketing outlays to launch the product or service (you may need $5 million or more in the first year to launch a new microcomputer software product).
- Other start-up costs unique to your venture.

How much of this can be raised from asset lenders, such as banks and leasing companies, by financing against inventory, receivables, equipment, real estate, etc.? Give rough estimates of amounts that can be bankable loans.

Most start-ups run out of cash before they secure enough profitable customers to sustain a positive cash flow. Your preliminary estimates should be within the amount an investor, a bank, the SBA or other lenders will be willing to commit to a single venture, or that you can personally raise. Are you convinced the amount is reasonable with respect to the venture's potential and risks? If other people are not convinced, what is it that you know they do not, or vice versa?

What are your preliminary estimates of manufacturing and/or staffing, operations and facilities requirements?

What are the major difficulties (equipment, labor skills, achieving quality standards) in the manufacture of the product, or delivery of the service?

How will you deal with these difficulties, and what is your estimate of time and money to resolve them and begin salable production?

It is quite easy to underestimate what it takes to overcome production and operations problems, and to deliver your product or service at a competitive price. If you or someone on your team is not experienced and competent in getting your product produced and out the door, you have a major gap to fill.

What is your best estimate of the prospects and time frame for realizing capital gain? What are industry price/earnings ratios, current valuations, future climate? Does the potential harvest justify the effort, risks and requirements?

Beware of compromising "forgiving and rewarding economics" in a venture you want to start. Life in a new venture can be exhilarating but very demanding. One way you can get the odds in your favor is to make sure the opportunity is attractive from an economic and financial point of view. Such opportunities are just the ones venture-capital investors, informal investors, and savvy entrepreneurs and managers will want to associate with.

Entrepreneurial Team Issues

The entrepreneurial process is people-driven. Successful investors consider the lead entrepreneur and the top managers to be the key to creating a successful, profitable business. Even if you do not seek venture capital, the relevant experience of the founders and their commitment is crucial.

Are the founders sufficiently committed to the opportunity? How much are they personally willing to invest and guarantee, and what portion of their net worth is it?

What know-how, knowledge of the industry and other skills are required for the venture's success? Do the founders have the relevant experience to execute the opportunity? If not, can managers be attracted to the venture who can fill the gaps?

Can the founders instill the necessary vision and entrepreneurial zest in new hires to sustain high performance and growth?

List the roles and contributions each founder is expected to make, and the anticipated salaries and ownership shares of each. (Equal salaries and stock ownership often indicate the team has been shaped on naive assumptions.)

Fatal Flaw Issues

Each new business has its risks and problems as well as its opportunities. No investor has seen a "perfect deal" as yet; very few are entirely clean of difficulties to be overcome, so it is important that they be identified as soon as possible. Much of the time the entrepreneurs can take steps early on to eliminate, or reduce negative effects from them.

What are the major risks and problems that you see in the proposed business? Indicate their order of importance. Consider especially the reliability of customer orders, their amounts and timing, sales projections, ability to achieve cost and time estimates, and the magnitude, intensity and vindictiveness of your competitors' responses. Time and again, first-time start-up entrepreneurs overestimate sales, are too optimistic about delivery dates, and underestimate the cost, effort and time required to reach a positive cash flow.

What are the significant trade-offs and assumptions that can affect execution or outcome? How severe are the negative consequences?

What can you do to minimize these considerations?

How do you rate the risk of the venture: high, medium, or low?

A recognition of risks and problems demonstrates to potential investors and prospective management-team members that the entrepreneurs are intelligent, realistic and know their business. Investors will assess their handling of them as significant indicators of their entrepreneurial ingenuity and resilience. There is nothing more damaging to the new-venture proposal than the discovery by investors, a lender, or a prospective partner of negative factors that the entrepreneurs did not know about, did not want to discuss, or cavalierly dismissed.

Idiosyncratic Issues

Are there any other vital issues or considerations, unique and situational to the nature of the opportunity and proposed business? Each venture—the founders, the timing, the situation—is a unique and specific set of circumstances. Not all issues can be covered in the screening guide that are pertinent to every venture. You will need to adjust and adapt for those particular idiosyncrasies here.

The opportunity guide should enable you to determine whether you want to continue and to develop a complete business plan. If you are able to complete the guide with mostly positive results, then a business plan is worth doing. If you and your partners are confident you are on the right track, then keep going.

8

Using Resources

Entrepreneurs who are successful do things differently than many managers in large organizations. One is their approach to committing or gaining control over resources in the pursuit of opportunity. In large organizations pressured by a trustee or custodial viewpoint, the attitude often is, "Do we have enough resources (including a cushion) to weather the tough times and not fail?" The attitude of the entrepreneur is, "How can we accomplish more with less?"

The entrepreneurial approach involves "bootstrapping," or minimizing the investment in people, money, and other assets. The key to bootstrapping is leveraging your own "sweat equity" and using OPR—Other People's Resources. These "other people" include outside investors, friends, relatives and business associates, who—along with some customers and suppliers—are willing to invest or lend money, lend people or phone lines, or provide free or inexpensive space or equipment. The trade-off may be friendship, favors, shared profits, future services, or some combination.

In one company that grew to $20 million in sales over ten years, the founders began with $7,500 in cash, along with liberal use of credit cards, and they have not had to raise any additional equity capital. Doing "more with less" included the founders themselves: As the company grew, the professional managers who took over the founders' old jobs admitted that it took two people to do the job of each founder.

Many entrepreneurs insist that the worst thing that could happen is to have too much money at the beginning. Some real success stories were launched in 1979-81, a time of miserable economic conditions and sky-high interest rates. Discipline and wisdom often come more readily when money and resources are tight.

Howard Head, famous for developing the metal ski, insists that had he raised all the money he needed to begin with, he would have failed by spending it all on one of the early, wrong versions of his ski. Instead, he worked up only a few pairs of skis at a time, and went through forty experimental models before he found one that worked—and before he ran out of money.

Howard Stevenson of the Harvard Business School sees the entrepreneurial commitment of resources as one step at a time, rather than all at once.[1] This reduces the exposure of the entrepreneur himself and spreads the risk among other people.

Why do successful entrepreneurs take this approach? They know they must respond quickly to be competitive. They know that decision widows are narrow and close rapidly. The entrepreneur thrives on such constant flux, and knows that it is very difficult to predict accurately what is needed to execute an opportunity. The flexibility gained from piecemeal commitment of resources can be one of those "unfair advantages" that entrepreneurs always seem to create for themselves.

In the early stages of a venture, successful entrepreneurs want to *control* and *use* resources, but are not obsessed with *owning* them. As Howard Stevenson put it, "All I need from a resource is the ability to use it. There are people who describe the ideal business as a post-office box to which people send cash."[2] In large organizations, control and use is assumed to require ownership, so that decisions center on how resources will be acquired and financed rather than used.

Many examples of control and use without ownership are to be found in real estate, where even the largest firms use the services of outside architectural firms project-by-project. The same is true of using the expertise and resources of outside law firms, consultants, design engineers and programmers.

1. H. H. Stevenson, "A New Paradigm for Entrepreneurial Management," Division of Research, Harvard Business School, 75th Anniversary Entrepreneurship Symposium, Boston 1983 (*Proceedings* 1985).

2. From a talk to the 128 Venture Group, Boston 1983.

One microcomputer software company was started up by a group of programmers and technical people. Their plan called for $300,000 in development money. How did they propose to deploy it? They wanted use half of it to buy a large computer. Leasing or borrowing or using slack time at night on someone else's, did not appeal. The result? Despite an excellent business plan, they were unable to attract venture capital. They did raise $150,000 from informal, private investors, but returned it because it was not enough to execute their plan, which included asset ownership.

Would a more entrepreneurial team have figured out an alternative way to keep going? I think so.

Why does the principle of minimal resources work for entrepreneurs? It reduces risk and lowers fixed costs, which favorably affects breakeven. And it lowers the cost of choosing to abort. Contrast that posture with the bleak prospects facing the owners of the now bankrupt Seabrook, New Hampshire, nuclear power plant.

Minimal resource commitment also lowers the risk of owning obsolescence. No wonder computer leasing caught on early and has prevailed, especially with entrepreneurs, given the rapid change rate in that technology! Once a system is bought and installed, you are stuck with it. Given the flux and uncertainty of market and technology in which most entrepreneurs must survive, the inflexibility of ownership can be a curse.

Decisions to lease or buy are not, of course, always simple, given the many complications, including tax issues. Also, variable costs do rise as fixed costs drop. However, if the entrepreneur has selected an opportunity with forgiving and rewarding economics, there should still be ample gross margins.

Larger firms often envy the resilience and quick response of smaller entrepreneurial firms. What is behind this envy? Minimizing commitment of resources allows trial-and-error testing of ideas. How many times have you heard an entrepreneur say, "Try it. If it works, keep going."? Imagine doing this if you own all the assets and resources of a business facing rapid change in markets and technology, such as computer graphics, fiber optics, or telecommunications.

A final note about OPR: The notion of the lone entrepreneur thriving by personal, singular effort is not only a myth, it is misleading. New entrepreneurs pursuing that notion may not appreciate the interdependence necessary to make a venture succeed. Reflect on the multiple constituencies that are part of a successful venture: investors, key staff people, customers, suppliers, creditors, and outside professional advisors, among others. The most productive sources of these players are the entrepreneur's networks and circle of contacts.

9

Choosing Consultants

You have some savings, an idea for a new business, and some relevant technical expertise and experience. But you know you need a partner who understands the marketplace better than you do.... You have a small business you run with a checkbook and the cash in a shoe box. You want to borrow some money, but your banker is unimpressed with the checkbook stubs and the shoe box.... Your $1 million specialty business has stable sales but a limited product line. You want to find new products that would fit in, but you don't know how to go about it.

These situations are typical of many would-be and existing entrepreneurs. To whom can they turn for help? What quality of help can they expect to find, and how much will it cost? Unfortunately, nowhere among small business resources are the choices so numerous, the quality so variable, and the costs so unpredictable as in the area of management consulting.

There are 40,000 to 50,000 private consultants around the country, a number growing by 2,000 or more annually. About half work alone; the others in firms of up to several hundred people each. Government agencies—mainly the SBA (Small Business Administration)—can provide consultants to small businesses. Some are paid by the government, and some volunteer. Various private and nonprofit organizations provide assistance to entrepreneurs. Business professors at colleges and universities also consult, in some cases privately and in others via federal programs.

Unfortunately, anyone can hang out a consulting shingle. A good number of self-promoters are only interested in making a lot of money; other consultants are skilled and can be invaluable. The trick is to distinguish the quacks from the legitimate experts. And avoiding the frauds isn't all. Entrepreneurs must have a clear idea of what they expect a consultant to accomplish. If they cannot communicate comfortably and effectively with the consultants they hire, they may wind up paying for a final report that only decorates the office shelf.

As if choosing and using a consultant is not tough enough, entrepreneurs face huge variations in cost. While the quality of most services at least roughly correlates with their prices, not so with consultants. The SBA, which is free, may provide advice more valuable than a well-known firm charging $50,000 to $100,000 for a minimal study. In between are consultants who will work for $100 to $1,500 a day and up.

There are ways to limit the choices and minimize the dangers. For one, the financial pinch on a start-up business may dictate using low-cost educational or government-funded programs rather than high-priced private consultants.

For another, consultants tend to have specialties. Know what kinds of problems you want help with, and you can quickly eliminate wrong choices. Even if you cannot pinpoint the exact problem, but simply feel the need for an unbiased and fresh look at your business, it is a good idea to fix on the broad area—personnel, manufacturing, or marketing—before seeking out a consultant.

What kinds of problems can consultants best help solve? The types vary between start-ups and going businesses. The *start-up business* usually needs help with critical one-time tasks and decisions that have a lasting impact on its chances of success; for example, assessing business sites, evaluating lease and rental agreements, setting up record and bookkeeping systems, finding business partners, obtaining start-up capital, and formulating marketing plans. Getting sound advice on these matters can be the difference between success and failure.

The *existing business* tends to face ongoing issues, many of which are special enough that outside advice is helpful in resolving them: for example, computerizing routine business tasks, deciding to lease or buy major equipment, devising appropriate benefit and compensation plans for employees, and changing inventory valuation methods. Settling these and other issues appropriately can clear the way for new stages of growth.

Once you have decided to hire a consultant, be hard-nosed and through in making your choice. Identify three or more candidates and interview them. Ask them to detail their expertise and approach. Then ask the one or more who are most impressive to prepare a proposal for handling the problem(s) you want help with. Ask for the names of other clients you can call for references—and follow through by calling them!

Once you have made your choice, work out a written agreement specifying responsibilities and objectives, along with type and amount of compensation. Like other outside experts, consultants charge an hourly rate, a fixed fee, or a retainer.

The qualities of the ideal small-business consulting firm are

- A "rolled-up shirt-sleeves" approach to the business's problems.
- Consideration for the feelings of the manager and his subordinates.
- A modest and truthful offer of services.
- An ability to produce results.
- A reasonable and realistic fee.
- A willingness to maintain a continuous relationship.

The hard part is finding the right consultant for your particular needs. Most entrepreneurs underestimate the time it takes to find one who has not only the right know-how but also the right chemistry.

Not long ago I sent the CEO of a rapidly growing medical technology firm to two consultants who worked with emerging, high-potential firms. Both had excellent reputations. The deciding factor was chemistry. When the CEO was asked what he learned from the other clients of the consultant he hired, he said, "They couldn't really pinpoint one thing, but they all said they would not consider starting and growing a company without him!"[1]

1. For a good discussion of the selection and use of outside professional advisors, see Howard H. Stevenson and William A. Sahlman, "How Small Companies Should Handle Advisors," *Harvard Business Review*, March-April 1988.

10

Should You Have Outsiders on Your Board?

Deciding to have outside members on the board of directors and deciding whom to chose are among the most trouble-some of decisions for entrepreneurs. If your firm is a corporation, you *must* have a board of directors, elected by the shareholders. If you raise venture or other outside capital, in all likelihood the investors will require that they be represented on your board.

The board elects the officers, but as long as you own or control the voting shares of your company, the choice of officers is yours. Complications can arise if you have to give up more than half your shares to raise capital. Unless you can accept this, think twice about raising venture capital at start-up.

In deciding to have outside directors, a number of considerations deserve careful thought. Doing so requires greater disclosure of operations and finances than you are accustomed to. Once you take the plunge with outside directors, it hard to pull back to your original position. Thus, you should start with people you know, who are close enough to be trustworthy, yet distant enough to objective.

Typically, most entrepreneurs ask their lawyers, bankers, or insurance advisors to be the first outside director. They should first ask themselves, "What does the business need?" and then seek the right person.

Most start-up companies go through various strategic windows: raising capital, securing customers, resolving technical issues and producing quality goods, adding key people, coping with rapid growth, and so on. Identifying these key strategic tasks helps answer the question: What additional expertise is needed and what relevant experience is missing from my venture that a director could bring?

Risks and Pitfalls

Once you have decided to include outsiders, finding the appropriate people for your board is a challenge. Many of the right ones are increasingly cautious about getting involved in new or emerging ventures because of the legal liabilities directors face in most states. Directors can be held personally liable for the actions of a company or its officers—for example, voting a dividend that makes the corporation insolvent, in some states voting for a loan out of corporate assets to a director or officer who defaults on it, or signing a false corporate document or report.

If directors act in good faith, they are excused for their involvement in such actions. In start-ups, acting in good faith may not be easy. It can be complicated by a novice management team, financial weaknesses and cash crises that tempt management to cut corners, and a lack of corporate information and records to use as a basis for judgment.

To make matters worse, outside stockholders may have unrealistic expectations that lead them continually to pester the company and the board. Experienced directors also know more time is required and the risk is greater for a venture with $8 million in sales than for one with $35 million. If all this were not enough, in many areas a climate of litigation threatens nearly any reasonable action.

One solution is indemnity insurance for officers and directors. But the entrepreneur must then ask, "If the risks are that bad, do I need the director in the first place? Or is the director so averse to risk that I won't get the kind of commitment to the company I want?"

Compensation and Informal Boards

The compensation of directors can vary widely. If you are serious about attracting a top-notch director, you are asking for at least four days a year for quarterly meetings, each likely to require another day of preparation; at least one more day for a wild-card meeting to cope with sudden fires; and various phone calls along the way. Fees for this investment of time might run $5,000 to $20,000 per year.

Advisory boards and quasi boards can be a useful alternative to outside directors. Such informal boards can bring needed expertise without the legal entanglements and formalities of a regular board, nor the complications and embarrassment of formally removing someone who is not useful. Informal advisors are usually much less expensive: they commonly get honoraria of $500 to $1,000 a meeting.

Finally, an informal group of advisors can be a good way to see a number of people in action and later ask one or two to serve as regular directors. Such a courtship allows both parties to assess the fit and chemistry before a formal commitment is made, and can prevent difficulties and possible litigation if things do not work out.

11

How Important is Legal Advice?

What do entrepreneurs need to know about law and lawyers? You may feel that you can barely stand to live with legal assistance, but you are doomed without it. John Van Slyke, an entrepreneur who has taught at the Harvard Business School, recommends that "... to manage relationships with lawyers effectively, entrepreneurs must know what lawyers do and how they think. Prudent businessmen and women do not wholesalely delegate legal matters to their lawyers, nor do they allow their lawyers to make many decisions for them. After all, the important signatures on contracts, tax forms, and other legal documents are those of the principals, not the lawyers."[1]

Here are some areas where you are well advised to seek competent legal advice.

• Form of organization (such as Subchapter S); the rights and obligations of officers, shareholders, and directors; what a quorum is; who can call a directors' or stockholders' meeting.

A founder nearly lost his company to maneuvering by the clerk and another stockholder. They plotted to call a directors' meeting at which they controlled the votes, and oust the president. He found out, and managed to get his own meeting called first, at which he controlled the votes, where he regained control by not re-electing the two dissident directors.

These things can happen. The entrepreneur must be aware of what he could be getting into when thick legal documents are dismissed as "just boilerplate."

1. J. Van Slyke, "What Should We Teach Entrepreneurs about the Law?" Division of Research, Harvard Business School, 1983.

• Contracts, licenses, leases, and agreements, particularly noncompetition employment agreements and agreements governing the vesting rights of shareholders and founders.

One entrepreneur hired a lawyer who specialized in the sale, lease and licensing of software. Without the subtle but powerful protections devised by both the entrepreneur (such as internal clocks that shut down the software from time to time) and the lawyer, the entrepreneur would have lost over $200,000 in uncollected fees and $2.5 million in a sale of the business.

• Intellectual property protection: patents, trademarks, copyrights, and privileged information.

• Current SEC, state, and other regulations concerning the securities of the firm, both registered and unregistered, and the advantages and disadvantages of different share instruments. The long-term consequences of violating a securities law are too great to take chances here.

• Real-estate transactions. Most entrepreneurs at one time or another will be involved in real-estate transactions, from rentals to buying and selling property.

• Tax implications and changes. A word of caution: The tail of tax avoidance too often wags the dog of good business sense. It's tough to find and bring off an opportunity to create a good business making a good profit. Look for opportunities to make money, not lose it for a tax shelter.

• Bankruptcy law, options, and the forgivable and nonforgivable liabilities of founders, officers, and directors. Some entrepreneurs choose not to prepay such federal and state taxes as unemployment, social security and workers' compensation so they can use the cash in the business. They assume that if they go bankrupt, the governments will be out of luck along with other creditors. Right? Wrong. In fact, the owners, officers and often directors are held personally liable for these obligations even though the company has gone under.

These are the core concerns for which legal advice is important. Fortunately, there are a growing number of attorneys in many parts of the country who specialize in new ventures. The best people to ask for a recommendation are your entrepreneurial peers, accountants, bankers, and associates. Or

- Ask other successful entrepreneurs for their suggestions.

- Look up the name of a venture capital firm[2] in your area that does start-up investments. Call one of their general partners, and ask for a recommendation.

- Call one of the Big Eight accounting firm offices nearest you, and ask for the partner in charge of the privately owned and emerging business group.

- Call your local or state bar association.

- Call a professor of entrepreneurship at a nearby college or university.

A word of caution. Lawyers should not make business decisions for you. They are usually so concerned about providing "perfect" or "fail-safe" protection that they are totally averse to risk. They will discourage you from any bold action. The entrepreneur must decide the odds of an unsavory event happening, the probable consequences, and if those consequences can be withstood or reversed.

Fortunately, most entrepreneurs do take advantage of legal advice. Almost all small companies rely on outside counsel, and a majority of attorneys consider small-business clients to be important.[3]

2. One source is *Pratt's Guide to Venture Capital Sources*, 13th ed. (Venture Economics, 1989), available in most libraries. Also available in most larger libraries is the *Martindale-Hubbell Law Directory*, a national listing of lawyers.

3. Of 5,000 companies and 5,000 lawyers surveyed. See "You and Your Attorney," *INC.* magazine, June 1982.

What factors enter into selecting a law firm or attorney? According to the *INC.* magazine survey cited here, over half the companies are influenced by personal contact with a member of the law firm, followed by reputation and a prior relationship with the firm. Equally revealing is that fee was mentioned by very few. Legal advice is not a resource to be "penny wise and pound foolish" about. Also, you should pick an attorney with the experience and expertise to deal with the particular issue you face.

An entrepreneur relocating his office to condominum space in a renovated historical building did not use the two who handled his other affairs. Why? Neither had experience with the complicated tax and muliple-ownership issues that arise in office condominum deals involving historical properties.

Last, as with partners and investors, the chemistry must be right, or the association won't work.

How are attorneys used? That depends on the needs and size of the venture, but newer firms use them mostly for contracts and agreements, personal needs of top management, incorporation, and formal litigation. Contracts and agreements are the predominant use, regardless of the size of the venture.

What about compensation and fees? Most attorneys are paid by the hour, though retainers and flat fees are more frequent among larger ventures; and the amount rises as the firm grows. Data from the INC. survey suggest that if you grow to $5 million in sales in the first five years, you will have legal fees of around $30,000. Have you included legal fees in your business plan?

If your venture has high promise, many law firms will defer charges and offer a lower rate at first to get your business, expecting to have a bigger client later on.

12

Selecting an Accountant

It is hard for entrepreneurs to fully appreciate accounting and what it can do for them. In fact, many tend to view the accountant as a bean counter, a sort of scorekeeper sitting on the sidelines, rather than as a player on the first team. This is a great mistake.[1]

How do you find the right accountant for you? Virtually all the major accounting firms have discovered the client potential of new ventures, a big plus for entrepreneurs. The basic choice is between a smaller local firm, one of the four to eight regional firms, or one of the Big Eight national firms.

• Evaluate the levels of service and attention offered. Some of the Big Eight, especially Ernst & Young and Coopers & Lybrand, have sought to excel in providing to privately owned and emerging businesses quality services beyond plain vanilla audit and tax work, plus their great depth of resources in tax and special areas. Local firms also can provide excellent service.

• Match your current and developing needs against the accounting firm's competence. The larger firms are likely best for complex, technical problems and now also can deliver top notch general business advisory services; the smaller firm also provides general management advice but usually lacks the technical depth and worldwide network of offices.

• Consider the cost. A partner in a large firm may charge almost twice what a partner in a small firm will charge, but you should not assume that the smaller firm is less expensive across the board.

1. Gordon Baty, *Entrepreneurship for the 80s* (Reston 1982).

• If your market and customers are national or international, the Big Eight firms can provide you with access to networks, resources and even potential customers well beyond the local or regional domain.

• If you plan eventually to go public, establishing a track record with a series of audits from one of the larger firms is preferred.

• Again, and perhaps most important, make sure the chemistry works.[2]

Probably the best source for an accountant is another entrepreneur who has found a good one. Other sources include bankers, attorneys, and trade groups. For new firms with great ambitions, using a Big Eight firm from the start can make a significant difference. An entrepreneur who built a seven-unit franchise into the nationwide leader of the industry described why he selected a Big Eight firm to assist his company from the start:

Bringing on [a Big Eight firm] was the best money we ever spent. As a new company we were in uncharted waters. The partners and young people are so bright, they hire only the best. They were interested in seeing us succeed.

At one point in time we were in a crisis caused by rapid growth and weighing two offers, one to sell the company, the other to bring on another major investor. [Our accounting firm] was able quickly to develop an analysis of the two offers and help us evaluate our alternatives. They had the experience and the expertise to meet our needs, and the capacity to do it almost overnight.

Also, acquisitions were a major part of our strategy. We needed a firm that could be looking at deals in Denver and Chicago at the same time. The talent and networks of [a Big Eight firm] are worth the money.

Once you have reached a significant size, you will find yourself in a buyer's market, but be wary of the lowest price and "freebies." As in most things, you tend to get what you pay for.

2. N. C. Churchill and L. A. Werbaneth, Jr., "Choosing and Evaluating Your Accountant," in Growing Concerns, ed. D. E. Gumpert (Wiley 1984).

One firm had grown to about $5 million in sales and would reach $20 million in the next five years, with ambitions to go public eventually. It distributed a brief summary of the firm, with background and track record, and a statement of its needed banking and accounting services.

The founders were startled by the aggressive response from several banks and Big Eight accounting firms. The firm changed banks and accounting firms, lowered their costs, and feel they are better served in the bargain.

Some accounting help is available free from booklets and other information put out by Big Eight firms. For instance, Ernst & Young offers *Guide to Preparing a Business Plan* and *Going Public.* Deloitte, Haskins & Sells puts out such booklets as *Raising Venture Capital,* and Price, Waterhouse has an excellent summary of the latest changes in the tax laws relevant to entrepreneurs. Ask for them when you call the head of the privately owned and emerging business group at one of these firms.

13

Entrepreneurs in Action: Chasing Geese

The unsuccessful entrepreneur's stumbling block is often the successful entrepreneur's opportunity. Dry runs can help you deal more confidently with some of the situations you and your venture will face. Based on entrepreneurial examples from real life, with comments on what was learned, what worked and what didn't, and how the iterative process can improve the odds for venture success, this and the following chapters show how the three essentials of venture creation—opportunity, people and resources—come together to face the difficulties which arise.

Anatomy of the Iterative Process

Athletes have found that they can improve their performance by "imaging," or thinking through the steps of their event beforehand, and "seeing" themselves performing successfully. Entrepreneurs can do the same thing by mentally going through the steps of start-up and operation before they actually do it.

Actual practice also provides learning. A study of twenty-four technology-based ventures showed a marked difference in performance between twelve first-generation ventures and twelve second-generation ventures.[1] "The creation of a first generation technology-based enterprise (called a spin-off) occurs when an entrepreneur starts a business to commercialize technology transferred from a previous source of employment. As the new firm develops, it in turn, becomes a source of technology and entrepreneurs for a second generation spin-off and so on." (Ibid, p. 36.)

1. Lawrence M. Lamont, "What Entrepreneurs Learn from Experience," *Journal of Small Business Management*, vol. 10, no. 3 (July 1972), pp. 35-41.

Chapters 13–17 are derived from material originally prepared by Alexander L. M. Dingee, Jr., for *New Venture Creation*, 1977.

Each second-generation venture was far more product-oriented than its first-generation counterpart. The second-generation venture also had a more balanced team, greater initial financing, higher sales in the first year, reached profitability earlier, and had significantly higher profits in its most recent year of operation. This performance indicates, as might be expected, that a venture team learns from experience.

If a would-be entrepreneur does not have much applicable experience, it can be very hard to start up and succeed with a new venture. But even unsuccessful attempts to start a venture build up knowledge of how to do so successfully.

The following history describes one entrepreneur's actual early, unsuccessful attempts to start a business, and illustrates what he learned from these attempts.

Struggling to Find a Venture: Five Goose Chases

An incipient entrepreneur named Charles received a Bachelor of Science degree in business administration with a minor in engineering. He knew he wanted eventually to start a business, but first he wanted to strengthen his engineering abilities. So he went to work as an engineer in the development laboratory of a chain-belt manufacturer, the CB Company. He thought he would be working on new-product development, which would provide him with experience directly related to starting a new venture. However, before he could do this, he spotted a need in the company for an automatic inspection machine for chain links and successfully proposed to the laboratory director that he develop such a machine for CB's use.

Goose 1. While working on the inspection machine, the laboratory director and Charles, who were graduates of the same school, discussed the possibility of Charles' starting a company to manufacture a chain-link testing instrument that had been developed by the director. With little data they decided that the market for the instrument was not large enough tosupport a small company. They did not seriously consider developing an integrated line of chain-testing instruments and handling tools, to create the business volume necessary for a viable venture.

Goose 2. Charles also had venture discussions with Bill, a shop foreman who had worked his way up from machine-repair mechanic. Bill was very skilled at grinding-machine set-ups and special machine alterations. Charles and Bill spent many hours trying to identify a product that would capitalize on the skills of the foreman. However, the two were unable to define a product that would meet any generalized grinding machine need.

Goose 3. Charles also had venture discussions with Tom, a clever mechanical engineer at CB Company. They talked of possible products based upon mechanical technology to tie in with Tom's unique design capability. Charles' father, a physicist, was also queried about products, and he said, "Tell me what the market needs and I might be able to design a product to fit that need." Charles and Tom were unable to identify a potential product or need because they had no detailed knowledge of any marketplace.

Goose 4. Charles, Tom, and an electrical engineer, Carl, then tried to come up with ideas. They decided they needed a place to work and began fixing up Carl's chicken coop for this purpose. Ten months later, the engineer had a nicely fixed-up chicken coop, but the team had no ideas for business. The work on the chicken coop had effectively taken ten months of effort away from the primary goal of finding an idea that met a market need.

Goose 5. Two years after Charles' first attempt to identify a venture opportunity, he was drafted into the army. At this time, Tom suggested that the team—Charles, Tom, and Carl—design some kind of electromechanical toy. Tom was an exacting craftsman and, as a hobby, had worked on model cars and planes and was adept at automobile repair.

After much discussion, the field of powered model cars or planes was chosen—based upon Tom's experience in building models. A car and a helicopter were picked first, and the car was given priority on the basis of Tom's love and knowledge of cars and the potential difficulty in making a working, powered model helicopter.

Charles and Tom agreed that there must be a market for a properly designed powered model car with the right price. This supposition was based only on the knowledge that model cars and toy trains sell in enough volume to support a fair-sized industry.

With no market data, the team began to design a model-car product based upon their own feelings as to what the consumer wanted. Charles and Tom provided all of the drive to build a prototype. Carl made a significant contribution to the design of the electrical control.

About ten months after conception of the idea, with the part-time effort of Charles and Tom, a prototype of a model car was completed. It consisted of a single eight-inch-long model car powered on a restricted track. Both speed and steering were controlled outside the car. The design appeared to be simple enough to allow low-cost manufacture. With a successful prototype completed, Charles and Tom decided that they would either try to license it to an existing manufacturer or start a business to manufacture and sell it.

Charles and Tom tried to find somebody with applicable venture experience to discuss how to start a company in the toy field, but failed to find any sources of good advice. Charles attended a large toy manufacturers' sales show in New York to size up the industry. The competitive rat-race image obtained from viewing two hotels full of toy exhibits and from two days of discussions with toy company representatives left Charles feeling that he wanted nothing to do with starting a company in the toy industry. Further, Charles and Tom both felt completely inadequate to go into large-scale production and consumer distribution. It was obvious to them that only by licensing the car model to a toy manufacturer could they realize a return from their efforts.

Charles made appointments to display the prototype car model to the Lionel and A. C. Gilbert companies, both manufacturers of toy trains. The chief engineer of Lionel said the concept was interesting and that an excellent job had been done in reducing the concept to practice. However, a corporate policy decision had been made at Lionel to get out of the toy field and go into government contracting.

The A. C. Gilbert meeting went better. The
happened to be meeting that day and became interes
Several of its directors drove the car around the tra
hugely enjoyed themselves. However, there was a powered mod
project already underway at Gilbert. Despite this, Charles and Tom were told that if they added a second car to their track, there would be a definite possibility of interest from Gilbert.

At this point, the team members had serious doubts about putting any more effort into the project. Putting a second car on the track was likely to involve much complicated work. Further, it was not at all certain that A. C. Gilbert would really be interested, or that a valid patent could be obtained to protect the idea.

Charles was now seriously considering a sixth venture (three years after beginning his venture attempts). Although Tom agreed to go further in developing a two-car system, the priority he set on this task was so low that no further progress was made.

What Was Learned?

After five goose chases, Charles had learned that for him it was necessary to have a partner to provide a balance of abilities in a venture effort. He had also identified some of the complementary abilities he needed in a partner and was aware of the necessity for high quality in these abilities.

Akin to team considerations were those of business contacts. Charles had learned that he had no business contacts from which to get advice. He was convinced that any future venture creation effort he made should include systematically expanding his business horizons and contacts.

A further conclusion was the importance of choosing the right business field. Charles now realized that an entrepreneur must pick a general field of business that appeals on a personal basis (the toy field had not appealed), one to which he or she can make a significant contribution (this had worked for the toy field), and one requiring skills the entrepreneurial team has (the team did not have the production and marketing abilities to handle a toy venture).

The major lesson learned from the fifth goose chase was that by moving step-by-step toward defined goals, two inexperienced individuals had been able to develop a workable product prototype. This prototype attracted favorable attention from the top management of two leading companies. To Charles, this was coming within shouting distance of success, and served to build his venturing self-confidence. Based on all the lessons learned, Charles was convinced that he could use his remaining ten months' time in the army to get a venture started.

14

A Goose is Caught: Birth of Massey-Dickinson

Would-be entrepreneur Charles initiated an army transfer to a quiet quartermaster corps laboratory in Boston. He was assigned to a job that required a Ph.D. in mechanical engineering, completely beyond his training. He could neither learn the job nor design a meaningful research program in his final eight months of army time. Charles therefore decided to use his remaining time in the service to start a business. In his new venture effort, he was determined to use everything he had learned from his previous efforts.

A Business Field is Selected

Through library research, Charles identified industrial instruments as a growing field. Through thinking about what was around him, Charles identified medical equipment and supplies as a second area of interest. Boston, a noted medical research center, seemed an ideal place to base a venture dealing in new medical products. This idea quickly flowered and took precedence in Charles' mind because the thought of working in a field where he would be helping humanity appealed to him.

Library research showed that the market for medical equipment and supplies was large and growing rapidly compared to other markets. Profit margins in the industry were above average. Charles visited various medical supply houses and determined that much of the instrumentation, equipment, and specialized medical furniture could be improved.

From talking with people at the supply houses, Charles found that many of the companies manufacturing medical products were small. Therefore, Charles felt that he could start small and be successful. There were existing channels of distribution for medical products that a small company could use, again showing Charles that a new medical venture could establish itself through these channels. Charles and Tom agreed that an effort to develop a medically oriented business on a spare-time basis looked acceptable. Carl was not included because of his previous lack of effort after an initial investment of a few hours.

The Business is Designed

Neither Charles nor Tom were fitted by their experience for starting a company. Each had only developmental engineering experience with the CB Company. They had no experience in marketing, production, finance or in medical supplies. CB Company had sales of $110 million per year so it was not a small-company experience.

At first it seemed they did not have much to work with. Charles listed the assets they had available:

Charles' ability to live on his wife's pay and his army pay for the six months while he was getting a company started.
Tom's willingness to work evenings at no cost to the venture.
Savings of $12,000.
Ability of Charles and Tom to design mechanical and electromechanical devices.
Proximity to large numbers of active medical records.
Proximity to the technological resources of Boston—libraries, consultants, machine shops, electronics manufacturing facilities, etc.

Charles decided to offer the one ability he and Tom had—design of devices—to the medical research community, so that they would be building on their expertise. Their proposed company would design special medical research instruments upon request. After completion of a design, the company would subcontract the manufacture of the instruments to eliminate the capital cost of equipping a shop and to retain manufacturing flexibility.

The design and subcontracted construction of the instrument would be done for a fixed price, agreed with the customer before work was begun. They anticipated building many instruments only once, but with occasional repeat orders. Selling services appeared to Charles to be a low-risk, low-profile way of entering the field, using the experience of the team as advantageously as possible.

Charles Takes Some Planned Action

Charles visited a well-known senior scientist at MIT who had some contact with the medical research field. The scientist encouraged Charles to proceed with the medical instrument business. He gave Charles the names of several medical researchers. He also mentioned that his son had just been through starting a successful company and might give him some useful tips.

Charles visited the son, Jack, who was very helpful. Jack gave Charles the name of a subcontract machine shop that he used, and the name of his corporate lawyer. Charles visited the corporate lawyer, who agreed to handle the new firm's legal needs. He recommended that the new firm be a partnership to avoid incorporation costs until it was determined that there was a market, that significant sales were possible, and that a method of limiting personal liability was needed.

Charles visited one of the medical researchers recommended by the MIT scientist. The doctor was located in the Warren Research Building of the Massachusetts General Hospital. The doctor, upon hearing of Charles' design service, asked if he would be interested in designing and building a new muscle-fatigue measuring instrument, based upon an old instrument. Charles agreed to return with a proposal. The doctor encouraged Charles on the need for the service he was providing.

Charles visited the second medical researcher, who also encouraged Charles about the need for special instrument service and recommended a subcontract machine shop that he might use.

The Massey-Dickinson Company is Born

As a result of the conversations described above, Charles and Tom decided to go ahead. They now needed a company name. They felt that the name must sound solid and established because doctors are conservative. After many hours of thinking, the name Massey-Dickinson Company was chosen. (Massey was Charles' middle name and Dickinson was Tom's last name.) The name sounded like Becton Dickinson, a company in the medical field, and Massey Ferguson, a company in the machinery field, both suggesting, subliminally, substance and longevity. Individuals' names seemed also to give some personal substance to the company—and the company initials were MD.

More Venture Actions are Taken, along with the First Order

With five months of army time left, Charles began accelerating his effort. Massey-Dickinson calling cards and letterhead stationery were designed and printed, a telephone answering machine was attached to Charles' apartment telephone, personal contact was made with a local bank, potential subcontracting machine shops were visited, and quotes were obtained for construction of the muscle fatigue instrument. Then a large number of hours were poured into readying a proposal for that instrument.

Charles submitted the proposal to the doctor, including a three-dimensional drawing of the proposed instrument. The price quoted for the design and complete instrument was $4,500. (The cost of manufacture, exclusive of engineering, overhead, and profit, was estimated at $3,400. The entrepreneurs had decided to "buy" their first contract to give them some experience.) The doctor gave them a purchase order for the instrument and Tom began making final drawings, while Charles selected the subcontractor and ordered parts.

The Business Becomes Real and So Does the Work

As Charles' time in the army came to an end, he became swamped with the details of supervising the construction of the machine, and with visiting more researchers at the Warren Research Building to obtain additional work. His apartment was close to the army laboratory and a ten-minute drive from the Warren Building. Charles made liberal use of army leave time, three-day weekend passes, evenings, and long lunch hours.

Almost four years after Charles initiated his first efforts to launch a venture, Massey-Dickinson Company was in business. Its first order was nearing completion, several additional proposals had been submitted to doctors at the Warren Building, and many customer discussions of future orders were under way.

A few months after leaving the army, Charles decided that a professional image required an office, so he arranged to rent office space from a subcontractor. He felt that being close to his major manufacturer would allow work in progress to be monitored closely. Massey-Dickinson now had an established air about it, with telephone, calling cards, letterhead stationery, office, a full-time employee, customers, and a book of pictures showing the several completed and delivered instruments. At this point, Charles was very enthusiastic, putting in a great many hours per week and handling everything from sweeping the floor to purchasing, subcontract management, engineering, bookkeeping and selling.

Apart from the rush of productive work on medical equipment, Charles was meeting many other venture milestones at the same time—equipping and moving into office space, hiring a part-time bookkeeper, arranging for typing service, incorporating the partnership, choosing a board of directors, getting product-liability insurance, making up a brochure describing the medical-equipment development service, broadening his contacts with subcontracting shops and with engineers who could provide backup design services, hiring a mechanical engineer, strengthening his contacts with his bank, and developing a business plan for raising needed equity money.

Massey-Dickinson Teaches Some Lessons

At the end of the first year, the company was loaded with work on special medical instruments. Charles had hired a disabled mechanical engineer and was also able to draw a small paycheck of his own from the company. Tom continued to work evenings for no salary. He enjoyed the engineering work as a hobby, but was turning out to lack the entrepreneurial drive necessary to create a going business. He enjoyed the security of a larger company. Charles knew he needed to find suitable team members, but he did not have much to offer. In the meantime, he was extending his experience and range of contacts, and the Massey-Dickinson Company was becoming an established company in the medical instrument field.

Charles Takes More Planned Action

As Charles' reputation grew, he saw that his business volume of about $20,000 per month could be increased over the next year to support two or three professionals. To expand further would require a service or product with a larger market potential.

Charles decided to analyze all the special medical products which had a sizable market. Eight were identified: neurological tools, test-tube handling equipment, cardiographs, medical pumps, medical furniture, programming equipment, data-processing equipment, and animal cages.

Charles invested significant time in market testing each area. The method was simple. Generally an order could be obtained for one item in the area of interest; e.g., a special data integrator. The product would be designed to meet the needs of a more general market. The price obtained would generally defray the cost of manufacture. The engineering design was done on a shoestring. The products were market-tested by a variety of means—from free new-product releases in technical journals to papers presented by the involved and interested researchers who were buying the equipment. The proof of the market test would be interested potential customers and sales.

A year and a half of product development was expensive. A bank debt approaching $200,000 based on inventory, work in progress, receivables, and Charles' signature forced Charles to pick the best-looking product and push it into the marketplace.

More Business is Defined and Started

Charles picked behavioral-programming equipment to push into the marketplace. This equipment is used to program psychological or physiological tests on humans and animals. The product was an advanced computer-type approach to an old product. The original equipment, built in a laboratory, had been market-tested at a major scientific meeting with good results. Many scientists wanted to buy it or see a catalog. Product design was completed at the same time that orders were being taken from local researchers and a catalog was being written. Charles selected an electronics subcontractor to build the equipment.

Charles, a medical research doctor, an electronics technician from a medical laboratory, and the engineer/subcontractor became an entrepreneurial team. Charles was the general manager, Charles and the doctor did systems design, the doctor tested the equipment and made a list of potential buyers, the electronics technician did application engineering and became sales manager, and the subcontractor carried out engineering (on speculation) and manufacture. The work described above may sound simple, but an immense effort was expended to bring the product to market in time to meet the demand.

The product was sold through display at four scientific meetings a year, selected customer visits, and direct mail. The doctor described to Charles how other companies sold their equipment in this field. Massey-Dickinson followed suit. Existing companies in the field had sales of up to $8 million per year—thus defining the market size. Charles felt able to cope and had a sales method he could control. Also, the market niche was not large enough to attract major competition. The unique solid-state character of the Massey-Dickinson product gave it a strong edge over existing equipment.

It was possible to develop the market with a reasonable amount of capital by leaning on the subcontractor to carry inventory and conduct engineering on a speculative basis. Approximately 30% of Massey-Dickinson was sold to raise the equity capital necessary to introduce the new product.

Charles Finds Out

From the experience of launching Massey-Dickinson, Charles learned a number of specific things. He learned how to

Start a business using subcontractors to maximum advantage.
Select subcontractors.
Manage subcontract work.
Bid complicated jobs accurately.
Engineer a variety of instruments and equipment.
Make business contacts.
Build banking relations.
Deal with customers.
Make progress according to a venture action plan.

In addition, Charles had acquired considerable general knowledge, including:

- Knowledge of managing an entire business, which required the integration of many factors in each management decision.

• A broad range of specific knowledge of market-study techniques, use of free new-product releases, generation of data sheets, exhibiting at trade shows, management of sales representatives and distributors, handling of customers, engineering and management of engineering, management of subcontractors, accurate costing of proposed products, use of patent attorneys, debt and equity financing, use of corporate attorneys, and use of consultants to broaden technical approaches.

• Through repeated use of subcontractors, how to select good subcontractors and maximize use of their facilities and assets.

• How to identify a market niche within a large and growing field that fitted his psychological makeup and skills. The small size of the niche allowed him personal contact with major customers, direct sale to the end user, and reward for high technical performance, which is easily recognized in a small field.

• Techniques for analyzing a potential niche: determining the size of the niche from the size of the existing companies in the niche, establishing that niche customers are easy to define and reach, and knowing some friendly potential customers in the niche.

• Reinforcement and refinement of all his previous learning. For example, he had learned more about the timing problems concerned with taking step-by-step action toward meeting a goal. In short, he learned that during the early stages of a new venture, the entrepreneur should not set goals so rigid that they prevent him from responding to actual market feedback. But, on the other hand, the entrepreneur must find and identify his basic goal and put all his energy into its development; at least until a secure base of sales is obtained.

• A sense of the dynamic, demanding, and interdependent nature of the goals in a venture action plan. The requirements involved in meeting venture goals come in an unending, demanding stream. He found that the requirements might change even as he worked to fill them. Most of the goals and their requirements were interdependent.

15

Another Goose is Caught: Geodyne

Charles, the entrepreneur of Massey-Dickinson Company, was busy developing his new behavioral programming equipment when a small job he had done at Woods Hole Oceanographic Institute suddenly provided a new opportunity.

A scientist at Woods Hole had purchased a single instrument from Charles. He wanted Charles, at no cost to Woods Hole, to develop a production design of this instrument in return for an order for twelve instruments. The scientist claimed that there would be a market for the instruments to other oceanographers.

Conversations with other oceanographers at Woods Hole and with two fisheries' laboratories suggested that there was potential for the instrument and a need for other ocean instruments. Further, the staff at Woods Hole said that there were significantly increased funding levels available for oceanographic research using such measuring instruments. Charles could see the beginnings of a new business with the allure (to him) of the ocean.

With two hours work in the library, Charles discovered that the federal government purchased large amounts of equipment for ocean research. Woods Hole represented a significant ocean research customer actually asking him to develop and supply equipment. Starting a second major business effort would dilute effort on the behavioral programming equipment—but it was not sure of major success.

The Dilemma Resolved and Venture Resources Defined

The behavioral programming equipment was well along in development, using the subcontractor. The Massey-Dickinson sales manager could make all the sales trips the company could afford. The medical one-of-a-kind business could be tapered off faster than planned, which would free a considerable amount of Charles' time and allow him to develop the oceanographic instrument business.

The major problem to be met if an oceanographic equipment business was to be started was the need for increased engineering capacity and on-site shop facilities of impressive size. Woods Hole would not buy major equipment from a cellar operation. If this problem could be solved, it was a potential advantage because it would keep out all other cellar shops from competition. The behavioral programming equipment subcontractor's facility was electronically oriented with no mechanical shop capability. Further, the facility was unimpressive. The five-man machine shop used for the medical one-of-a-kind work was not up to producing a volume of electromechanical and electronic instruments, and had no engineering capability.

Charles picked a large machine shop he had used before, owned and run by a father-and-son combination—both engineers. The shop itself was in a modern, well-organized building. The machine shop owners agreed that the Woods Hole instrument order could be taken under the name of Massey-Dickinson. A rough plan of action was laid out for sharing of work load, development and use of capability and resources, split of potential ownership, and criteria for market evaluation.

The gratis engineering work was to be split between the machine shop and Massey-Dickinson. The shop would charge normal rates for its work, and any profit would be split equally between the two groups after the shop's work was paid for. The shop facility could be shown to Woods Hole as available for meeting their needs. The shop would also handle the project's telephone calls. If a real market were identified and proven by sales to Woods Hole and other groups, a separate company would be formed, with ownership split 50–50 between the two companies as partners.

The Product Developed and a Company Formed

A good, reliable instrument was developed by Charles and his new partner, Fred, and produced by the shop. To make one of the components for the instrument, a special timing device was searched out, tested, and imported in volume from Switzerland. This device was altered and calibrated in the machine shop. It performed a timing function not filled by any commercially available component.

Ten months after receipt of a $35,000 purchase order, the instruments were delivered to Woods Hole, and they made a good impression. There was particular interest in the unique timing component. After testing, Woods Hole placed an order for 100 of the timing components at $240 each, to be used on another instrument. These components worked well, and one of the Woods Hole program managers suggested that Charles and Fred could make the timer and other components for a new type of instrument that Woods Hole had developed and was testing.

Six months later, Charles and Fred decided to form a company on paper. Manufacturing would still be done in the machine shop, but the company would have a name, letterhead, calling cards, and a symbol. This move kept the financial commitment low, while presenting a better integrated image to the customer.

The oceanographic equipment business was a secondary and pleasurable undertaking for both Charles and Fred. It was decided to create a glamour image to go along with the glamour of dealing with the ocean. This approach helped foster a flexible attitude in the partners that was a definite asset in laying out the venture action plan.

Company Image and Operations

After much effort, a company name was created—Geodyne Corporation. This name was specific enough to indicate the type of field, but not limiting to the expansion visualized. Fred designed a company symbol that placed the letters G E O D Y N E within a world globe form. The design looked so good that an advertising artist did all the graphics necessary for the letterhead, business cards, labels, and data sheet format for a very small fee so that he could carry them in his portfolio.

An incorporation was initiated, with stock split equally between Charles and Fred. Since Charles had identified a potential instrument business with live customers and had instrument-manufacturing experience, and Fred had a shop facility that provided instant credibility to those customers and he also had some instrument experience, the two partners seemed equal in what they were contributing to the venture.

Geodyne developed a data sheet on the timing device, using a format drawn up by the advertising artist, and printed it on the copying machine. Later, it was printed as a two-color data sheet. At this time, Woods Hole asked Geodyne to start supplying major parts of a new instrument that Woods Hole had developed and had been making itself. Now orders or these instruments and the first instrument designed by Geodyne began to flow in from other institutions. Oceanographers at these institutions had heard papers presented by Woods Hole scientists and had seen the instruments demonstrated at Woods Hole.

Keep That Best Customer

Charles and Fred realized that instruments in use at Woods Hole were Geodyne's best salesmen, and that Woods Hole was crucial to early venture success. However, the Woods Hole staff felt that Geodyne should be located near the Institute to service Woods Hole needs properly. Yet, Charles and Fred did not want to lose the many venture resources available to them near Boston, and it would be inefficient if 90 miles separated them from the plant facility.

As a compromise, Geodyne, with sales still under $500,000, opened a small technical office next to Woods Hole in a half-basement of the Woods Hole Inn. The neat office was artistically furnished at low cost and equipped with one each of the instruments and mechanisms Geodyne was selling. Further, copies of data taken by Geodyne instruments and plotted by Woods Hole were displayed, along with photos of the instruments in use at sea and photos of the interior and exterior of the machine shop. In short, the office looked functional and businesslike. It created an atmosphere of success and gave an image of the major operation existing in the main facility in Boston.

To man the office, a third partner, Paul, a personable ex-Woods Hole oceanographer and electrical engineer who lived nearby, was put on Geodyne's payroll at a small salary. The concept of a technical office manned by a professional oceanographer near Woods Hole kept the Institute as an excellent customer. Oceanographers visiting Woods Hole and perhaps staying in the Inn could stop by the office and talk shop and business.

The day the office opened, a government official attending a technical meeting at Woods Hole walked into the office and said that his agency, the U.S. Public Health Service, wanted to buy what amounted to $3 million worth of equipment! However, it was obvious to Fred and Charles that it would be necessary to prove that Geodyne was more than a paper company in order to close the sale.

More Resources

On the basis of the potential order, a successful entrepreneur, Jack, who had recently founded and built a major scientific product company, agreed to join the Geodyne board of directors. The seasoned Boston lawyer for this entrepreneur's business also agreed to be on the board. At this time, a building belonging to a company that had gone bankrupt came up at auction.

It was located directly on Route 128, and as a result, had significant visibility. The machine shop was only 500 feet away. Charles, Fred and Pete agreed to bid on the building and they got it for $600,000. The team felt that this move would give substance to Geodyne as a company capable of producing $3 million worth of equipment. They also felt that the risk in buying the building was low because the price was low, and a building directly on Route 128 was a reasonably liquid asset. And even if the Public Health Service contract did not materialize, space within the building could be sublet until company sales volume grew to the size capable of supporting the full building.

At the bankruptcy auction of the building, the team picked up at a bargain price some desks, file cabinets, chairs and workbenches. Several pieces of equipment developed to build Woods Hole instruments in the machine shop were moved into the newly acquired building. The work to be moved from the machine shop was assembly, testing, packing, shipping, engineering, sales, and administration. All these factors made it possible to equip the plant for a small capital investment. A sign painter was hired and the Geodyne symbol was constructed on a four-foot by six-foot sign and mounted on the Route 128 side of the building. The exterior and interior were now assuming a going, businesslike image.

At the start of business, a few individuals were shifted from the machine shop payroll to the Geodyne payroll, and several new people were hired. Since the work to be conducted in the building was low-skill assembly, it was not difficult to hire the people needed. The idea of going to work for a company manufacturing oceanographic equipment had a lot of appeal to many of those hired.

The bank that had serviced both the machine shop and Massey-Dickinson over a number of years had been kept up-to-date on the progress of Geodyne and its oceanographic equipment. It provided a mortgage for the full purchase price of the building, treating some small improvements that Geodyne made in the building as the down payment. The bank also agreed to give references to the Public Health Service.

Capital equipment and money were necessary to progress further. Charles, Fred, Pete, Paul, and Jack all invested varying amounts in Geodyne. Charles had to find $50,000 to hold his ownership in Geodyne at the level he desired. To do this, he went more heavily in debt to the bank. The bank allowed him to do this because it believed Geodyne had a tangible value.

The bank was pleased with Charles' and Fred's decision to go full time in Geodyne. Fred's decision was easy to make—leave a partnership in a job shop for an ocean products company with the option to return to the job shop if all did not go well. Charles felt the dynamic potential of a field just starting, and the romance of manufacturing products related to the ocean, fitted his personality better than the more stable and established behavioral equipment field. After trying to run Massey-Dickinson on lunch hours for several months, Charles was able to convince the behavioral programming equipment subcontractor to become president of Massey-Dickinson on a full-time basis and merge his company with Massey-Dickinson.

Problems

The Public Health Service required that the data from the Geodyne instrument be handled automatically or no contract. This required a very complex automatic reader that Woods Hole had been going to develop but had never started. The development of such a device was no minor undertaking. Paul, the oceanographer, worked full-time on finding a subcontractor to do this very specialized job while Charles worked on developing an in-house machine.

To Charles, it rapidly became apparent that building a data-reading machine could never be accomplished in time to win the $3 million dollar contract. Paul did find a company selling a general-purpose computer with optical input that could be altered to read the data. He convinced theyoung company of the excitement and promise of the field and the long-term future of Geodyne. The machine alteration required a very expensive type of movie projector. For the demonstration to the Public Health Service, such a projector was rented, torn apart, and fitted into the system. With several 24-hour work stints, the reading technique was demonstrated to the satisfaction of the Public Health Service.

More Problems

The Public Health Service put out a request for a bid on Geodyne-type equipment and Geodyne submitted the second-to-lowest bid. The lowest bid was rejected because it lacked automatic reading. The contract was awarded to Geodyne—and then taken away one month later because of political intervention by the low-bid competitor.

However, the Public Health Service fought hard to overcome the political pressure. They were willing to fight because the instruments were proven in use and because Geodyne projected a successful, businesslike atmosphere that left them feeling that delivery, quality, and performance promises would be met.

The full $3 million contract was reinstated two months after it was canceled. Delivery was completed successfully over a period of 18 months. This contract gave the company the resources to develop a series of new products and services.

Geodyne built a full team of entrepreneurs, managers, and skilled engineers. Production, at the outset, was managed by non-equity owning employees who later received stock options. The company became predominant in the manufacture of buoy-mounted oceanographic instruments. It also successfully provided data processing services based upon its instrument capabilities.

The merger with a larger company expanded its services into environmental data collection. Prior to the merger, company sales were just under $7 million per year. Seven years after the merger, its total sales of oceanographic instruments and environmental data collection services were approaching $25 million.

Interrelationship of Venture Components

The machine shop became interested because of the product potential from Woods Hole. Woods Hole became interested in large volume production from Geodyne because of the involvement of the machine shop. The outside directors were interested in being involved with Geodyne because of its potential for success based on major orders. The largest of these orders was partially dependent upon the company's demonstration of corporate strengths, such as a good board of directors.

The order also depended on automatic data-reading ability. The data-reading subcontractor made a major effort to demonstrate an ability to read and process data because of the potential of the contract and the belief that Geodyne could successfully supply over $3 million worth of equipment, though the company's sales had been less than $500,000 the year before. The subcontractor's belief in Geodyne came from the customer's belief in Geodyne, which partly came from the contractor's capability.

The very brief history of Geodyne does display a number of venture components that were utilitarian but created high value. One year after Geodyne had moved into its building, a very conservative brokerage house offered to take Geodyne public at a valuation of $10 million. The venture components of marketplace, contact with customers, existing contracts, sales growth, profits, location, Woods Hole office, and quality of team undoubtedly entered into the evaluation. In any case, it is nice to be wanted, but the team refused the offer because they personally did not need liquidity and the company was financing its development and growth from profits and bank debt.

By careful selection, Geodyne obtained attractive but pivotal venture components at reasonable cost, e.g., the name Geodyne, the Route 128 building (which appreciated severalfold), the Woods Hole office, and the entire product line. Presenting a crisp, consistent image of a competent winner helps relations with customers, banks, suppliers, and stockholders. Perhaps most important is the positive effect of the new company on paid employees and on the entrepreneurial team. Very often, if you think you are successful, you are successful.

16

Problem Solving

Once started, a new venture usually demands far more time from the entrepreneurial team than was predicted or is possibly available. To understand this, imagine yourself in the following situations:

- The manufacturing space being rented by your venture proves to be inadequate, and new space must be searched out, altered, and a move made.
- The product brochure being turned out is far harder to write than was envisioned.
- The major potential customer demands a far more detailed instruction and service manual than was expected.
- The telephone company can't give you enough lines.
- The sales manager quits and a new one must be recruited.
- Three important customers in different parts of the country want equipment demonstrated right away, but a major defect has just been discovered.
- The price on a component for the product has been increased and the delivery time extended four months.
- Your spouse broke a leg skiing.

Time pressures can easily force an entrepreneurial team into a fire-fighting mode, where all its time is spent responding to crises. Therefore, it is worthwhile to try to anticipate what major problems may be encountered in the venture, so that standard operating procedures can be used to deal with crises. Beyond this, the team, when aware of what typical operating problems may arise, can be thinking about solutions or contingency plans. That way, the problems when they occur will not cause a major psychological shock.

Some Things to Watch Out For

No matter how organized a group is, some problems will suddenly appear, ranging from a minor thorn in the side to a full-blown crisis. It may be difficult to recognize or identify these problems in the hurly-burly of day-to-day operations. Listed below are practices and issues that sometimes lead to trouble.

• Pricing too low. A start-up team is always nervous about getting customers, so there is a tendency to underprice. In a team, the marketing and sales people will want to succeed at their function and a low price will help. Making a profit at that price must be confronted by someone else.

A start-up company in the capital equipment business had a product better than the best on the market. The entrepreneurial team priced it just under their competitor's best product to make sure it would sell. However, the team also felt they would have more orders than they could handle.

The team was convinced by outside consultants to price the product above the competing price because this would establish by price that their product was best. More important, it would hold down the number of orders to what could be produced, while increasing company profits.

The entire profit on the company's second-year sales was the margin by which they had been convinced to raise their prices, adding significantly to their total capital and reducing the need for further investment.

• Overly enthusiastic sales projections. It is often hard to believe that a customer will not buy what or when he said he would. A mistake that entrepreneurs continue to make is their failure to realize that a customer may buy, but only half as much as he promised. Failure to discount sales predictions accurately can lead to bad profit performance and a negative cash flow. Also, the team believes its own sales story and forgets it must perform to succeed.

• Accepting new business. The venture should always build on what its team has already done. When the ratio of unknowns to knowns in a project gets high, the risk of failure increases greatly.

• Overspecifying. In a new field the customer often does not know what to specify for performance. If performance can be left vague, do so. In the capital equipment venture, several years went by with very little specification writing, partly because there was no time. Finally, after several new engineers had been added to the staff, a customer requested a bid with specifications on a new instrument. The engineers wrote a specification. The founder questioned the specification, and it was loosened. Even so, it was not met without far more work and cost than anticipated.

The overspecification concept can be carried to many aspects of the business: for example, when borrowing from the bank, don't promise more performance than you need to. The good feeling that you get from promising more than you need to buys you nothing. However, failure to meet your promise has significant negative implications in a banker's mind.

• Expecting too much from outside help. Outside part-timers can help, but don't count on them to make you succeed. It is unfair to expect a professional such as a lawyer or consultant to solve all your business problems for you. If a lawyer is good, he or she is being paid anywhere from $60 to $300 per hour. If ethical, he or she will try to minimize the time spent in getting your job done. The lawyer cannot take your problem home and mull it over for endless hours, as you would. You can expect sound advice and professional aid but not necessarily detailed creative solutions. If you have an unusual problem, expect to use the lawyer, accountant, and tax adviser as resources to provide you with the facts you need to solve your problem.

• Impulsive risk-taking. There are many projects your venture will undertake that present considerable risk to the venture if they do not succeed; e.g., a nonstandard system to be delivered on a tight schedule to a fussy customer. The potential market created by the new system is large, and the team thinks the advantages outweigh the risks. However, the investment you make in the system is based on the assumption that it will increase your annual sales by 50%. Failure to perform satisfactorily on the contract could jeopardize the financial stability of the company.

To identify possible problems beyond those that specialists are worried about and taking care of, try crying over your milk before you spill it. Imagine that the system has failed, and your company as a result is going into bankruptcy. Project yourself into this mode and role-play the part of the desperate entrepreneur. What do you feel went wrong? What should you have done to prevent the mistake? Who of the specialists working on the project should have taken what actions? Now come back to the present, count your blessings, and take those extra precautions.

This example was real. The entrepreneur in the case did try the spilled milk method, came up with the potential problem, but did not take action. The problem, a major one, did occur. The venture survived only after an expensive, agonizing effort.

• Cashing out instead of in. When your venture goes public or merges, don't be so pleased with the upcoming bonanza that you lose your objectivity concerning the details of the terms. Many people have made a fortune through hard years of work and lost a good part of it when they went public or merged. To a venture team, psychologically, the details often seem like unattractive paperwork to avoid thinking about. But remember, the stakes are high and there is more downside risk and more unknowns in a public offering or merger than in most of the dealings the team has gone through to develop the venture.

Getting the Most from People

The number of people necessary to make a venture succeed may be the hardest factor to monitor and manage, and other top team members are often a major factor in causing difficulties. Are you, as a lead team member, burdened with a lot of things that should never have reached your desk? A "yes" answer to this question may indicate worse than a lack of delegation on your part. It may be a reverse delegation from partners and subordinates who don't have a clear picture of company goals or policy, or are not capable of handling their positions—or worse, are willing to take it easy while you do all the work.

How do you, as a lead team member, feel about your work? Do you feel harassed or uncomfortable doing things you don't know how to do? Are you communicating well with your partners? Do you trust your partners' business skills, drive, ethics, need for power, and commitment to the venture? Doubts about any of the above can indicate that you, in relation to the team, and the team itself are not working to full capability.

Indications of this would be widely conflicting perceptions of the same event from different team and staff members, repeated inability to come to a consensus, lack of communication of critical information in timely fashion, subordinates making bad decisions, and subordinates making crucial decisions that should have been checked out with the lead entrepreneurs. The phrase, "we need a system for ... " may indicate you need a system, or it may indicate the person talking thinks the team is not meshing.

Another factor to consider is an absence of strategy meetings. This often indicates such problems as lack of communication, lack of trust between partners, or lack of recognition of day-to-day problems. If this condition exists over a significant period of time, it clearly indicates a team preference for operations and fire-fighting over planning and controlling the venture's direction and fate.

As we have seen, "do lists" are a powerful tool for use in moving the business step by step in the desired direction toward each of its goals. Lack of effective do lists on the part of any of the venture's managerial personnel is a warning light which should be heeded.

High employee turnover may be another indicator of low morale and a need for better communication. Sometimes the entrepreneurial team will expect too much from employees working for pay only, with no equity incentive. This expectation can cause frictions and high turnover.

In success, the entrepreneurial team should remain alert to the problem of arrogance. Business arrogance, or believing you have the key to success in your field, may be disastrous if conditions change. Technical arrogance may lead you into narrow products, dead-end streets, or obsolescence. Sales arrogance may leave you with some new competitors. Personal arrogance may add a spin-off from your company to that list of competitors.

Minding the Store: The Product

Does the venture's product or service work in the field under real conditions? The reasons for product failure should be verified to your exacting satisfaction. Misunderstanding the extent or cause of failure may lead to large unexpected overruns in development cost. Further, the cost of production may be more than expected, if the product can be produced at all. Knowing what it is up against at the time of first failures, the team could consider going in an alternate direction while the sunk cost was low and there was enough capital left to allow strategic choice.

Another mistake is simply having too many different products. In starting into a new field, a venture may rapidly develop products to meet different customer needs. When it is not apparent which products are going to be crucial to success, this is a valid strategy—if development can be done in spare time or the customer pays for it. However, at some point, there will be products that bring in little in sales, customer good will, or image, while they dilute management, sales, engineering and service effort and working capital. This dilution of resources must be watched closely because it is insidious. There will always be defenders of the broad product line, and objective analysis is necessary to keep a line in proper balance.

An endemic problem in small product companies is that of service or user manuals and documentation. A system should be set up to handle service manuals and documentation from the start of the venture. However, in reality this usually does not happen until forced by circumstances. It takes time and experience to write good documentation. If the product or service is unique or in a new, growing field, the user will often be lenient about accepting marginal documentation. As the field matures, standard requirements for documentation arise that must be met to compete effectively.

Corollary to the user product information is production documentation. When manufacturing is done in house, a new venture often operates with little documentation. The lack may only become apparent when an increase in volume forces the venture to subcontract. As in-house manufacturing grows, documentation also becomes crucial to individual and department communication and performance. Here the problem will show up as one of quality control.

Taking Care of Business: Sales and Customers

The life blood of the company is sales. This is so vital that booked sales must be one of the six or eight key variables monitored in some fashion. Do not accept excuses for why sales were not closed as predicted. Failure to close sales is a common problem in new ventures. Strategies must be developed to handle the problem immediately.

One company that failed to grasp and solve the sales closure problem received its necessary first major order after it had been irrevocably closed down.

Your company may have good sales but some irate customers. Those irate customers may know something you should know about your venture. Alternatively, one irate customer can do your company a lot of sales damage.

Financial Control

A new venture that is unexpectedly short of cash is, believe it or not, a sign that many entrepreneurs ignore. For example, many accounts receivable are overdue, but the team is too busy having fun developing new products to "waste time" doing the dirty work of pursuing accounts. Instead, the bank loan is increased. In such a case one person should be assigned to pay attention to collecting overdue accounts. A cash shortage may come from many causes and should be understood and corrected.

When expenses run higher than predicted, you should also get nervous. There may be underlying causes other than the obvious ones. The underlying causes may take time to solve; meanwhile, your expenses remain high.

Environment

Your venture exists in the marketplace and the world. If the economy is going down, the effect will eventually get to your venture no matter how insulated you think your business is. Watch out for interest rates going up, loans getting scarce, and accounts receivable stretching out as a result.

17

Strategies for Success

Some years ago, an entrepreneur was told in July by the director of a federal government agency that, with heavy fiscal pressures on the agency budget, it was extremely unlikely that the entrepreneur's venture would be funded for twelve months starting in January. This government agency was the only significant customer of the venture. The service being supplied was specialized, and until more operating experience was obtained it would have almost no other market—a calculated risk the venture had taken to achieve its long-term objectives.

The agency director's comments were disastrous news for the team. It looked as though more than two years of intensive work on a unique service would be halted, with grave implications for survival of the venture. As you can imagine, a lot of discussion went on in a hotel room that night.

The next morning the lead entrepreneur called the agency director and said that there were six possible directions to go to ease the government's funding problem for that product; and further, it seemed impossible that the government would want to stop funding a project which had had initial success and met significant needs of the government program involved.

The office director laughed at the persistence of the entrepreneur but invited the team back for further discussions that lasted all morning. The venture team convinced the director that before the end of the year meaningful indications of need for the service could be obtained, sources of supplementary funding lined up, general support from the director's constituency obtained, further positive product performance demonstrated, and a plan outlined for developing self-sufficiency.

A specific list of results which the venture had to obtain by December in order to retain its government funding was hammered out in that morning meeting. The venture achieved these results, was funded again, and has continued to provide a unique successful service since that time.

It is almost axiomatic that the entrepreneur believes he or she can control his or her own fate. This and other entrepreneurial characteristics (learning from failure, persistent problem-solving, goal orientation) allow a fast bounce-back when undesirable events hit the new venture.

In the case above, the venture team did not get knocked down psychologically upon hearing a bad prognosis from the government agency director. They believed they could influence their own fate by an immediate second approach to the government agency. The approach was: We can and will continue to succeed. Here is what we plan to do. Your agency can benefit if we succeed together. Which parts of our new plan are most significant to your agency? Can you help us if we achieve our plans in the next few months? This approach made it hard for the agency director to say "no" to an entrepreneurial team exhibiting determination, resourcefulness, and straightforward drive to continue working on a problem the agency needed solved.

The team was aware of the sales risk involved in dealing with a single large customer. The risk was heightened by pressures on the agency to cut funding. Therefore, the team was psychologically prepared for a funding cutoff, and had considered some possible methods of survival. Awareness of possible problems and preparing alternate solutions ahead of time is a mode of operation that should be applied by entrepreneurs to everyday operation. There are two parts to this mode: a vision of the future and total immersion.

Vision of the Future

A vision of the future is what pulls the entrepreneur through the daily details and problems that must be dealt with to get to the future. The ultimate goal of the venture becomes as real or more real to the entrepreneur than present-day life. There may be several models of this future world in the entrepreneur's mind. These models shift and change as actual data eliminates, confirms, or strengthens them. When present-day problems occur, the models may be looked at for possible solutions, to give confidence to the entrepreneur in making decisions.

For instance, recently an entrepreneurial team was trying to establish a price for a new financial management service. Normally, the fee charged would be 3 to 4% of the capital being handled, the same for groups that appeared to offer similar services. But the costs involved in supplying this proposed new service were too high to allow only 3 or 4% to be charged.

In group discussions, one of the entrepreneurs projecting a future model declared that the new venture being proposed was not a management service, but a development operation with a subsidiary management function involved. Therefore, past management-fee precedents did not bear on setting the fee for the new service.

Total Immersion

A corollary concept to future vision is total immersion. This concept is also equally valid for day-to-day operations and for long-range problem solving. Members of an entrepreneurial team will immerse themselves totally in their endeavor, its operation, the product, marketplace, venture environment, competition, current literature, innovations, etc. Total immersion works because, with enough intelligent hours applied, one mind or small group of minds can grasp all the essential details of an entire business and make accurate, fast and efficient operating decisions.

Larger companies generally do not deal in total immersion because it requires too much work and time on the part of paid employees. In place of this, the large company will use more people to attack a particular problem. Adding more people to a decision and and action process often means more factors involved, more complication, more time required to move, more reasons not to move, more chances for things to fall through the cracks, and ultimately higher overhead and prices. Thus, a motivated, capable, totally immersed new venture team can carve itself a place in the market based on its ability to make rapid, integrated decisions and take positive action in a timely and cost-effective way.

Total immersion must last long enough in a new venture to get the company going well and in a solid market position. Once it is established, total immersion is not as crucial, but many ventures continue to operate on it. Digital Equipment Corporation is now the second largest computer company in the world. Several of its founding entrepreneurs are still operating in a total-immersion mode nearly 30 years after its start-up, although they have been able to delegate major authority to new first-

and second-level management, many of whom also operate in a total immersion mode.

Problem-Solving Techniques

The Bandwagon Effect. To develop into successful businesses, most new ventures need good rapport with customers, suppliers, bankers, consulting professionals, and other business contacts. People dealing with a new venture are taking some risk. They like to feel that they are dealing with a winner. This impression comes through the team's ability to communicate it. Detailed knowledge of all aspects of the venture so that questions asked by outsiders get answered correctly and skillfully, and meeting goals on or ahead of schedule, all build credibility in the eyes of outside associates.

Creating the image of a winner builds a bandwagon effect that adds momentum to the new venture. Outside associates want the tangible benefits of doing business with a growing new venture and enjoy associating with success early enough to prove their ability to discern it. This requires that they jump on the bandwagon, which means they supply the new venture with scarce materials, loan the venture money, and buy the venture's products.

The bandwagon will sometimes move faster or slower than the venture, and the team may need to push it. For instance, it takes courage to be a first customer. It certainly does not hurt to hear about others who are considering purchase of the new product. With other customers thinking of jumping on the bandwagon, the bandwagon goes faster. To become the first customer, which is fun, one must now run faster to catch the bandwagon and get that first customer's seat. Therefore, a purchase decision that would normally have taken six months may take three months. The Geodyne put-together discussed in an earlier chapter is an example of the bandwagon effect.

Defining the Problem. Defining the problem correctly is a key factor in problem solving. Too often a symptom is defined rather than the problem itself. In the financial services case mentioned above, the symptom was inability to sell the service. An improper solution would be to look for a new set of customers. The problem was trying to sell in competition with financial management services viewed by the customers as similar to those proposed. The price was too high in that context. The answer to the correctly stated venture problem was to sell a new package (development plus financial service) at a new price to the same customers, rather than to look for new customers.

Using Time as Capital. Time for the new venture is like capital. Real dollar capital allows a wealthy venture to buy resources all at one time when needed. A continual flow of relevant resources and opportunities is going by any venture team all the time, like a conveyor belt. If the venture team can pick off resources as they pass by, enormous leverage can be obtained by combining these resources over time.

in the financial management service mentioned above, several specialized and talented individuals became available over a period of three years. They were used as client consultants. When the time came to place the full services product in the marketplace, these individuals were there, tested and trained in new techniques and adding greatly to the credibility of the venture.

Another way of using time as an asset is to gauge carefully when you need to commit to the solution of a problem. Don't always fall into the good manager syndrome—a problem to be solved should be solved immediately. For example, a common mistake often made by entrepreneurs is to create a corporation long before there is any commonsense need for it. This may forces commitments to bookkeeping, taxes, company name, equity distribution, and job functions long before necessary.

A problem itself may change over time, thus opening potential new solutions. An example of this is the venture with one government customer.

The team had tried to get a contract from a second agency, with no success. Then a new director of the second agency was appointed. He was somewhat more responsive to the venture. Now, because of change, there was an opportunity for solving a marketing problem.

Even with the change, however, it was difficult to come to agreement with the agency. The lead entrepreneur, after many go-rounds, handed the job to one of the other team members, who thought he could close the sale. Two months later a third member took over and carried it farther. Finally, a combination of two team members closed on a contract, two years after the original sales effort had started.

A change in circumstance over time, combined with the technique of tossing a discouraging job back and forth among close-knit team members, broke this difficult marketing problem. The team technique works for two reasons. One is that, with each shift, new energy is brought to the problem. A second is that new skills and personality may provide a new or better fit to the problem. (This team approach does assume that time is available for such shifting to be tried.)

Solving Problems Piecemeal. Solving a problem by using the time techniques is, in effect, stringing the problem over time or treating it in serial form. This, in turn, is a form of breaking a problem into pieces, which is a powerful problem-solving tool when confronting a seemingly insoluble, complex problem which must be handled in a fairly short time interval.

Take the easy parts first. Then try breaking the difficult parts into further pieces. If the pieces can be solved, try reassembling the problem and solution and look for dysfunctional effects. If these effects respond to additional solutions, you may have generated an integrated solution to the entire problem.

Role-playing. Another highly productive problem-solving tool is that of role playing. You imagine yourself in the role of a major or critical component of the problem. In the case of the financial management services company, the entrepreneurs role-played potential customers to check their acceptance of a higher fee for a unique package. This role-playing was carried over into the written rationale to be given to the customer. In another case, I role-played my competitors in a highly competitive bidding situation. My company won as low bidder by $5,000 on a $500,000 contract.

Solving Very Difficult Problems. The above techniques deal with the normal run of venture problems. What do you do with the really difficult problems? A venture problem philosophy that can occasionally reap large rewards is making a silk purse out of a sow's ear. Take the worst thing that happens to you and turn it to your advantage.

Charles, described in an earlier chapter, developed this philosophy when drafted into the army unexpectedly, breaking his career path. Since his time was being used inefficiently, he had a lot of spare time. In the second year of army duty, he arranged a transfer to a desired city. Weekends, three-day pass time, leave, nights and lunch hours were spent starting a medical instrument company. At the time of separation from the army, a field of business had been chosen, a strategic plan developed, a company founded, customers developed, and an order received and in process.

This silk-purse philosophy has been repeatedly proven successful. Business progress often consists of taking two steps forward and sliding back one. If some of the major slides back can be turned to major steps forward, a venture's progress can be smoothed and improved.

Index